family matters

A BIBLICAL PERSPECTIVE FROM DATING FEARS TO TWILIGHT YEARS

ARDEN TAYLOR

RIVERSTONE GROUP
PUBLISHING

Dedication

This book is dedicated to:

My loyal wife, Dianne, who is the love of my life.

My three daughters, Jennifer, Jill, and Jaren who brought joy to my home.

My three sons-in-law, Michael, Ross, and Jason who are Christian gentlemen.

My seven grandchildren who have given an added dimension to the word love.

My mom, Mary Taylor, who taught me about sacrifice and commitment to the family.

My granny, Shields Waller, who taught me about the value of the family.

My twin brother, Allan, who has been my best friend.

My mother and father-in-law, Dale and Wanda Fox, who have loved me like their own.

My Lord and Savior, Jesus Christ, who has made me apart of the family of God.

ISBN 978-0-9763092-4-6

Design and Production
Riverstone Group, LLC, Canton, Georgia

Manuscript edited by Kay Mitchell

Printed in Canada

Contents

To Tie the Knot
or
Untie the Knot?

What does the Bible say about marriage, divorce, and remarriage? When should we tie the knot, and when should we untie the knot? And if we untie the knot, what does the Bible say about marrying again? We need to understand what the Bible says about marriage because throughout Scripture it is used to describe the relationship between Jesus and the church.

We need to understand what the Bible says about these issues because virtually every family in America has been touched by divorce, and there is great confusion in our culture about marriage, divorce, and remarriage. If a church does not develop and communicate her theology regarding marriage, divorce, and remarriage, we further confuse people by sending out mixed signals and are inconsistent in our ministry.

A pastor may say one thing in premarital counseling that a Sunday School teacher may contradict in a class. There needs to be discipleship of both singles and marrieds regarding these important topics. Confusion runs rampant if we don't understand God's viewpoint on these subjects.

Marriage problems are not unique to our contemporary times. They have occurred throughout history. The church at Corinth was afflicted by this problem. It is to marriage, and some of the problems related to it, that 1 Corinthians 7 is devoted. Here Paul deals with the misconceptions and misbehavior of the Corinthian believers in regard to singleness, celibacy, and marriage.

In verses 1-7, Paul establishes the general principle that marriage is the norm for Christians but that singleness is a special gift from God and is good. In verses 8-16, Paul gives admonition and cautionary advice to four groups of believers regarding marriage.

1 Corinthians 7:8 But I say to the unmarried and to the widows: It is good for them if they remain even as I am;

9 but if they cannot exercise self-control, let them marry. For it is better to marry than to burn with passion.

10 Now to the married I command, yet not I but the Lord: A wife is not to depart from her husband.

11 But even if she does depart, let her remain unmarried or be reconciled to her husband. And a husband is not to divorce his wife.

12 But to the rest I, not the Lord, say: If any brother has a wife who does not believe, and she is willing to live with him, let him not divorce her.

13 And a woman who has a husband who does not believe, if he is willing to live with her, let her not divorce him.

14 For the unbelieving husband is sanctified by the wife, and the unbelieving wife is sanctified by the husband; otherwise your children would be unclean, but now they are holy.

15 But if the unbeliever departs, let him depart; a brother or a sister is not under bondage in such cases. But God has called us to peace.

16 For how do you know, O wife, whether you will save your husband? Or how do you know, O husband, whether you will save your wife?

Paul's admonition is to four groups of believers regarding marriage:

1. The admonishment to the unwed

Paul's cautionary advice for the SINGLE Christian

Paul said, "But I say to the unmarried and to the widows: It is good for them if they remain even as I am; but if they cannot exercise self-control, let them marry. For it is better to marry than to burn with passion." (1 Cor. 7:8).

These verses answer the question, "If I was married and divorced before becoming a Christian, can I remarry?" This question faced the Corinthians in Paul's day, and this same question is prevalent today. Are people who were once married and have been saved since their divorce now free to remarry?

Now, only single people can get married: therefore, let us first answer this question, "Who are single people?"

We find three different groups of singles mentioned here in 1 Corinthians 7. Understanding the distinctions of these three groups is essential.

A. Single people are virgins.

In verse 25 Paul gives instructions to the *"virgins,"* referring to those who have never been married. The word *"virgin"* used here is the Greek word "parthenos," and it means "unknown, or maiden." This is obviously referring to one who has never been married; in fact, one who has never known or been involved in a physical relationship.

Paul encourages *"virgins"* to remain celibate and single, but if they marry they have not sinned (1 Cor. 7:25-28).

There is a second category of single people:

B. Single people are widows.

These single people were formerly married, but that relationship was severed by the death of their spouse. We see the usage of the word "widows" in verse 8. The Greek word here is "chera," meaning "a widow (as lacking a husband)." This word is derived from the Greek word "chasma," which means "chasm or vacancy." A widow is lacking a husband because there is a chasm or gulf between them caused by death.

Paul encourages *"widows"* to remain single, but *"if they cannot exercise self-control"* they should marry (1 Cor. 7:9).

There is a third category of single people:

C. Single people are unmarried.

Who are the unmarried?

The word *"unmarried"* is found only four times in the New Testament, and all four usages of this word are right here in 1 Corinthians 7 (vs. 8, 11, 32, 34). This is the Greek word "agamos" and it means "unmarried." That doesn't seem to help us much, but this Greek word is derived from another Greek word, "gamos," and it means "nuptials, marriage, wedding." This *"unmarried"* person is one who was formerly married.

Verse 32 uses the word to refer to a person who is not married.

Verse 34 uses this word contrasting a *"virgin"* and an *"unmarried woman."* Paul is making a distinction between two different groups of women. Whoever the *"unmarried"* are here, they are not a *"virgin."*

Verse 8 speaks to *"the unmarried and to widows."* Again, Paul is making a distinction between two different groups of women. Some are *"unmarried"* and some are *"widows."* So we can conclude that the unmarried are not widows.

Verses 10 & 11 give us the clearest insight regarding who are the *"unmarried."* Paul says, *"A wife is not to depart from her husband. But even if she does depart, let her remain unmarried or be reconciled to her husband."*

The *"unmarried"* here is not a virgin or a widow. The *"unmarried"* refers to those who were previously married but not widows. Those who are now single but are not virgins. The "unmarried," therefore, is the divorced person.

Paul encourages those "unmarried," those who were formerly married, to stay "unmarried" so that they can can care "about the things of the Lord" (vs. 34). But what if the "unmarried" wants to remarry? Is this permitted?

This is a tough question, yet I think the answer is yes. However, let me say that I think their first and greatest effort should be to reconcile with their former spouse.

If you wrong someone before you were saved by breaking into their house and stealing their jewelry, don't you think it would be the right thing to go and make things right with that person now that you are saved?

In your former marriage, if you wronged your spouse, don't you think it would honor the Lord for you to make restitution and reconcile that relationship now that you are saved?

Here is yet another reason why I think many well-meaning Christians should not try to play matchmaker. Often times we don't know all the facts, nor do we always know the heart of a person. This is a dangerous game because you could tempt someone in an area that is not pleasing to God. God is the greatest matchmaker. Just ask Adam and Eve.

God is the greatest matchmaker. Just ask Adam and Eve.

Over the years, I've had people leave the church because I would not marry them, because at least one of them had an unscriptural divorce in their past. You see, if you're a Christian you are wrong to initiate a divorce for any reason except adultery. If you remarry, you close the door on the Holy Spirit to work in your heart, or the heart of your former spouse, to reconcile the marriage.

Marriage is not superior to being single, and it limits potential for serving Christ. However, Paul says a single believer who *"cannot exercise self-control, let them marry. For it is better to marry than to burn with passion,"* (1 Cor. 7:9). The only place we find this word *"burn"* is right here, and it means "fire, to be ignited, to be inflamed."

If a Christian is a virgin, a widow, a divorced person who divorced because their former spouse was guilty of adultery, or a divorced person who has been saved since they were divorced and does not have the gift of celibacy and is being strongly tempted sexually, he or she should pursue marriage. Because "it is better to marry than to burn with passion."

A person cannot live a happy life, much less serve the Lord, if he or she is continually burning with sexual desire, even if the desire never results in actual immorality. And in a culture like America where immorality and sexual innuendo are so prevalent and accepted, it is especially difficult not to succumb to temptation.

> *A person cannot live a happy life, much less serve the Lord, if he or she is continually burning with sexual desire, even if the desire never results in actual immorality.*

I believe that once a Christian couple decides to get married they should do it fairly soon. In a day of lowered standards, free expression, and constant sexual suggestions, it is difficult to stay sexually pure. The problems of an early marriage are not nearly as serious as the danger of sexual immorality. But remember, only marry in the Lord.

Tips for those looking for a mate:

1) The resolution of marriage

Don't shortcut God's principles regarding marriage. Resolve in your heart that you have no options outside of God's Word.

2) The risk of marriage

Anyone who wants to get married just for the sake of getting married runs a tremendous risk of marrying the wrong person. Marriage should be the result of knowing this is God's pick of a mate for you.

The first marriage was Adam and Eve's and they could honestly say, "You are the one God chose for me."

3) The restriction of marriage

The marital relationship is temporary in the sense that it is restricted to this life only. In heaven we will not be "given in marriage" (Matt. 22:30; Mk. 12:25; Lk. 20:35). Our greatest relationship is to Jesus. As believers we will forever be His bride.

If you are right with God and it is His will for you to marry, He will send the right person. To find the right person, be the right person.

To find the right person, be the right person.

4) The redirection until marriage

If you desire to marry, yet you have no potential candidate, while you're waiting on the Lord, redirect your energies. Keep your mind off of temptation. You should avoid listening to, looking at, or being around anything that strengthens the temptation. Two of the best ways are involvement in ministry and physical exercise.

5) The resistance until marriage

God will help you to resist temptation. Paul said, "No temptation has overtaken you except such as is common to man; but God is faithful, who will not allow you to be tempted beyond what you are able, but with the temptation will also make the way of escape, that you may be able to bear it" (1 Cor. 10:13).

6) The rejoicing until marriage

If you're not married, rejoice! God either wants to use you as a single or is choosing the right one for you.

2. The admonishment to the unfulfilled

Paul's cautionary advice for the SEPARATED Christian

Paul now gives advice to those who are married. "Now to the married I command, yet not I but the Lord: A wife is not to depart from her husband. But even if she does depart, let her remain unmarried or be reconciled to her husband. And a husband is not to divorce his wife" (1 Cor. 7:10-11).

Paul deals with two issues here:

A. The issue of divorce

Paul makes it clear that he is talking to Christian couples because he is giving them a "command." Paul never gave commands to the unbeliever.

So that there would be no doubt about his teachings here, Paul says that this was the teaching of Jesus. During His earthly ministry Jesus, in Matthew's gospel, quoted from Genesis 2:24, *"For this reason a man shall leave his father and mother and be joined to his wife, and the two shall become one flesh." "So then, they are no longer two but one flesh. Therefore what God has joined together, let not man separate"* (Matt. 19:5). In Matthew's gospel, Jesus was answering the disciples' questions. Jesus explained to them that God allowed Moses to permit divorce only because of the people's *"hardness of heart,"* and that it was permissible only in the case of sexual immorality.

Divorce is contrary to God's plan for us. As a matter-of-fact God says, *"I hate divorce"* (Mal. 2:16). Divorce is allowed only in cases of sexual immorality as a concession to the innocent party in irreconcilable cases of unfaithfulness. Yet even in cases of sexual immorality where there is REPENTANCE, there can be RESTORATION. I don't ever think we could ever say, "God led me to divorce my spouse."

Many divorces today are because of sexual immorality; however, many are not. "No fault" divorce laws have made divorce too easy today. People divorce because they are unfulfilled in their marriage or because they fell out of love. But let us note that love is much more than a feeling; it is a choice, an act of the will.

> *I don't ever think we could ever say, "God led me to divorce my spouse."*

The world has never seen such love as was demonstrated by Jesus on the cross. Based on the agony we see in Jesus in the Garden of Gethsemane, we must conclude that He was troubled about that which He faced. Thank God, He did it anyway!

Paul says that, "A wife is not to depart from her husband . . . And a husband is not to divorce his wife" (1 Cor. 7:10 & 11).

B. The issue of remarriage

Paul was not discussing divorce based on sexual immorality. He was talking about divorce for other reasons. We can be sure that some of the believers in Corinth were divorced; perhaps others were planning to divorce. To those people Paul says, "But even if she does depart, let her remain unmarried or be reconciled to her husband" (1 Cor. 7:11).

If a Christian does divorce another Christian, except for sexual immorality, neither one is free to remarry someone else. Paul says they are to live single or be reconciled to their spouse. In God's eyes that union has never been broken. Paul says that this is not his counsel, but a command from the Lord (1 Cor. 7:10).

3. The admonishment to the unequaled

Paul's cautionary advice to the Christian married to an unbelieving SPOUSE

Paul now gives us a word to the believer who is married to an unbeliever, *"But to the rest I, not the Lord, say: If any brother has a wife who does not believe, and she is willing to live with him, let him not divorce her. And a woman who has a husband who does not believe, if he is willing to live with her, let her not divorce him. For the unbelieving husband is sanctified by the wife, and the unbelieving wife is sanctified by the husband; otherwise your children would be unclean, but now they are holy"* 1 Cor. 7:12-14).

What are you to do if you are already married and your spouse is an unbeliever? Well, first of all, let me say that you married out of the will of God. Paul also said, *"Do not be unequally yoked together with unbelievers. For what fellowship has righteousness with lawlessness? And what communion has light with darkness?"* (1 Cor. 6:14).

What is a Christian to do who is married to an unbeliever? Are they free to divorce their *"unequally yoked"* spouse to either live as a single or remarry a believer?

Paul says that the teaching he is about to give was from him and not Jesus. Paul is not denying the inspiration of this Scripture; he is just saying that the Lord had not given any prior revelation regarding the "unequally yoked" marriage. For us to deny Paul's teaching here, and be consistent, then we must deny all of his other writings as well, which means we would have to deny most of the New Testament.

Paul instructs us that God views marriage in two ways:

A. God views marriage as a union.

Christians were not to worry that they themselves, their marriage, or their families would be defiled by the unbelieving spouse. Just the opposite was true. Both the children and the unbelieving spouse would be *"sanctified"* by the believing spouse. This does not refer to salvation. One's faith could never suffice for another. If it could the spouse would no longer be an unbeliever, but a believer. The word here means "to purify, to venerate." God would view this home as set apart for Him when one in that home is a believer.

There are many people whose name appears on the membership roll of the church but whose name does not appear in the Lamb's Book of Life. If God could use only churches where every person was a truly born-again, blood-bought saint, then God could use very few churches. A church where there are some believers is far superior to a church where there are no believers.

A home where there is a believer is far superior to a home where there are no believers. Unbelievers in the home are blessed because there is a believer in the home. The blessings that a believer experiences can spill over to others in the home. Hopefully, others in the home will be saved because of the life and witness of the believer. Over the years, many have been brought to faith in Christ through the testimony of a family member.

> *A home where there is a believer is far superior to a home where there are no believers.*

God told Abraham that He would spare Sodom if only there were ten righteous people there. And when ten righteous people could not be found, God did not destroy the city until Lot and his family had departed. God was willing to bless many wicked people for the sake of a few of His own people in their midst.

B. God views the family as a unit.

God looks on the family as a unit even if there is spiritual division. Every one in the family is blessed by the one who believes. Therefore, Paul instructs that if an unbelieving spouse is willing to stay in the marriage, the believing spouse is not to seek a divorce.

Paul says that if both parents are unbelievers, the children will be unclean, and guarantees that the presence of just one Christian parent will protect the children. It is not that their salvation is guaranteed, but that they share in the spiritual benefits of their believing parent.

If you have an unbelieving spouse, your testimony should be so clear that it can lead to the salvation of your children and possibly your spouse.

4. The admonishment to the unhappy

Paul's cautionary advice when an unbelieving spouse wants to SPLIT

Paul now instructs the believer what to do in the event that the unbelieving spouse wants out of the marriage, *"But if the unbeliever departs, let him depart; a brother or a sister is not under bondage in such cases. But God has called us to peace. For how do you know, O wife, whether you will save your husband? Or how do you know, O husband, whether you will save your wife?"* (1 Cor. 7:15-16).

What is the believing spouse to do in the event the unbeliever is unhappy and wants to dissolve the marriage? If an unbelieving spouse is determined to leave the marriage, Paul says that the Christian should not insist on their staying or contest the divorce.

Paul says, *"A brother or a sister is not under bondage in such cases."* The word *"depart"* used in verse 15 means "to be in space." Paul says to let them go as if they were "in space."

A marriage is dissolved only by:

1. The DEATH of your spouse (Rom. 7:2).

2. The DEFILEMENT of your spouse—sexual immorality (Matt. 19:9).

3. The DEPARTURE of your unbelieving spouse (1 Cor. 7:15).

When the marriage is dissolved in any of these ways, the Christian is permitted to remarry. Throughout Scripture, whenever divorce is permitted, remarriage is permitted.

If a Christian divorces another Christian, except for sexual immorality, remarriage is clearly forbidden because the bond of matrimony has not been broken in the sight of God. Jesus said, *"Therefore what God has joined together, let not man separate"* (Matt. 19:6).

However, if the bond is broken by death, adultery, or the leaving of an unbelieving partner, remarriage is permitted.

If the unbeliever cannot tolerate the spouse's faith and desires to be free from the marriage, Paul said, *"let him depart"* (1 Cor. 7:15).

Should you tie the knot or untie the knot? The only sure counsel comes from the Scripture.

A Promise Is Made To Be Kept

About half of our marriages, which started with promises made at the altar of a church, now end with the sound of the judge's gavel in the county courthouse.

What are the reasons for people getting a divorce? Communication breakdown, infidelity, constant fighting, emotional abuse, falling out of love, an uninspired physical relationship, spouse doesn't make enough money, physical abuse, falling in love with somebody else, and boredom.

After marriage, many have wondered if they made the right decision, especially in a culture where we have separations, divorce, live-ins, shack-ups, and homosexuality running wild.

Minnie Pearl once said, "Gettin' married's a lot like gettin' into a tub of hot water. After you get used to it, it ain't so hot."

Why are marriage promises being broken?

Let me answer that with six statements:

1. We have forgotten our commitment.

When you got married, you made a commitment to your spouse. Remember? I want to talk about something that's a little old fashioned . . . commitment!

A grandson asked his grandfather, "Grandpa, what did your generation wear for safe sex?" The wise grandfather replied, "A wedding ring!"

This throw-away, disposable culture knows very little, and understands very little, about commitment. We use something and then throw it away. Today we buy disposable cameras, take our pictures, remove the film, and throw away the camera. It seems as if our society has adopted this kind of mind set regarding the holy union of marriage.

What does a woman want in a husband? The following describes what every woman wants in the ideal husband:

> He will be a brilliant conversationalist. A very sensitive man - kind and understanding, truly loving and hard working. A man who helps around the house by washing dishes, vacuuming the floors, and taking care of the yard. Someone who helps the wife raise the children. A man of emotional and physical strength who is as smart as Einstein and looks like Robert Redford.

That's what every woman wants; here's what she usually gets:

> He always takes her to the restaurant, someday he may even take her inside. He doesn't have any ulcers, he gives them. Any time he has an idea in his head, he has the whole thing in a nutshell. He's well known as a miracle worker; it's a miracle when he works. He supports his wife in a manner in which she is accustomed - he's letting her keep her job. He is such a bore that he even bores her when he compliments her. He has occasional moments of silence which make his conversation brilliant.

What does a man want in a wife? The following describes what every man wants in the ideal wife:

> She's always beautiful and cheerful. She could have married movie stars but wanted only him. She has beauty that won't run in a rainstorm. She is never sick, just allergic to jewelry and fur coats. She insists that moving furniture by herself is good for her figure. She is an expert in cooking, cleaning house, fixing the car and TV, painting the house, and keeping quiet. Her favorite hobbies are mowing the lawn and shoveling the snow. She hates charge cards. Her favorite expression is, "What can I do

for you, dear?" She thinks he has an Einstein brain and looks like Mr. America. She wishes that he would go out with the boys so that she can get some sewing done. And she loves him because he is so sexy.

That's what a man wants; here's what he usually gets:

She speaks 140 words a minute with gusts up to 180. She once was a model for a totem pole. She is a light eater - as soon as it gets light, she starts eating. Where there's smoke, there she is . . . cooking. She lets him know that he has only two faults: everything he says and everything he does. No matter what she does, her hair looks like an explosion in a steel wool factory. If he gets lost, he opens his wallet and she will find him.

The Golden Rule of Marriage
What you want in your spouse, produce first in your own life.

Love is a commitment. Love is based on one's vow, one's word, one's promise. Feelings come and go, they rise and fall, they are frequent and infrequent. Commitment stays the same.

The Scripture is clear about vows.

"When you make a vow to God, do not delay to pay it . . . Better not to vow than to vow and not pay" (Ecc. 5:4-5).

There are two kinds of people: People of Convenience and People with Commitment.

Marriages that break up and quit do not break up and quit because their problems were more severe than marriages that stay together. Marriages that break up do so because they look for a way out, instead of a way to keep it together. If you're looking for an excuse to get out of a marriage, you can do that within one week of your wedding day. When you're looking, it doesn't take long.

People of Convenience...	**People with Commitment...**
1. Are emotion based. Ruled by their emotions.	1. Are character based. Ruled by character.
2. Ask, "What is easiest?" Always looking for shortcuts.	2. Ask, "What is right?"
3. Think, "When I feel good, then I'll do it."	3. Think, "I'll do it, then I'll feel good." Motion determines your emotion.
4. Controlled by moods. Moods control people of convenience.	4. Controlled by priorities. Is your life controlled by your moods or your priorities?
5. Have a selfish mind-set. Think of self.	5. Have a servanthood mind-set. Think of others.
6. Their life and lips disagree.	6. Their life and lips agree.
7. Look for excuses.	7. Look for solutions.
8. Are outwardly influenced Look for a way out.	8. Are inwardly influenced. Look for ways to keep it together.
9. Quit during tough times.	9. Persevere during tough times.
10. Are whiners.	10. Are winners.

If you're on the marriage freeway looking for an exit, you will find one. But marriages that last, and go somewhere, stay on course. If you are a person of convenience, if you are a person who is looking for exits, I am not only concerned about your marriage, I am concerned about your finances, your job, and everything else in your life.

Why are marriage promises being broken?

2. We have forgotten our covenant.

Solomon speaks about our companion and our covenant.

"Who forsakes the companion of her youth, And forgets the covenant of her God" (Prov. 2:17).

When you got married, you said something like this:

"I will love you, comfort you, honor and keep you, in sickness and in health, to have and to hold, from this day forward, for better for worse, for richer for poorer and, forsaking all others, be faithful to you so long as we both shall live."

You entered into a covenant. Don't forget your vows!

Did you hear about the two boys who attended a wedding? After the wedding, the younger boy asked the older boy how many women a man could marry. The older boy replied, "Why, sixteen, of course." The young boy wanted to know just how he knew it was sixteen. "Because," replied the older boy, "the preacher said, for better, for worse, for richer, for poorer? That's sixteen, right?"

The wedding vows themselves remind us that there will be some tough days ahead.

On the wedding day everything is so perfect. The bride has been pampered. She's had her hair done; she's had her nails done. She has on her wedding gown; he has on a tuxedo. She has her family and best friend there by her side. He has his family and best man there by his side. They are surrounded by singing, musical instruments, beautiful flowers, family, and friends. There is a reception afterwards with food. Everyone's in a gala mood. This is a very good day. If you can't feel a tingle on this day, you don't have a tingler. They walk out of church, go on their honeymoon, and a few months later wonder why they don't feel like they did on their wedding day. Who would? On your wedding day everybody pampered you and waited on you; it was your day! Surely you don't think the rest of life will be like this? Get real! Marriage is only for tough people who understand commitment, and wimps need not apply! If you are a quitter in life, don't get married! Because you'll not only mess up your life, you'll mess up someone else's life as well.

Robertson McQuilkin, former president of Columbia Bible College and Seminary, is a great example of a promise kept. When his wife Muriel was diagnosed with Alzheimer's disease, McQuilkin faced two divine callings: president of two schools and husband of Muriel.

He couldn't do both. He said it took "no great calculation" to resign his position and give himself to Muriel's care. He said it was a matter of integrity because forty years earlier he promised to care for her in sickness and in health. "She's such a delight to me," he said. "I don't have to care for her, I get to!" He said that when he made a promise, he made a promise. Robertson McQuilkin was a promise keeper.

A Christian marriage is an agreement, a covenant. A three-party covenant with each party agreeing to fulfill their part.

Marriage Is a Covenant Between Three Parties

1) God's Part

When you're a saved, born-again Christian you have the Holy Spirit living within you. Therefore, when you enter into marriage, you take God with you.

Marriage began in Genesis:

> "And the LORD God said, 'It is not good that man should be alone; I will make him a helper comparable to him.' Therefore a man shall leave his father and mother and be joined to his wife, and they shall become one flesh" (Gen. 2:18, 24).

What happened after God created Eve for Adam? She sinned! Yet, God didn't say, "Well, she messed up, I'll get rid of her and make you another wife." Just because somebody messed up, God isn't about to give up.

2) Woman's Part

The apostle Paul instructed married women,

> "Wives, submit to your own husbands, as to the Lord. For the husband is head of the wife, as also Christ is head of the church; and He is the Savior of the body" (Eph. 5:22-23).

Today, the feminist movement would make men and women so similar that one of them would be unnecessary. In fact, getting rid of men is one of feminist's goals.

Wives, your submission is not a sign of weakness. On the contrary, it is a sign of strength. In my position as pastor, our church staff ultimately answers to me. Does that make me better than they are? Absolutely not! As a matter-of-fact, I have less education that any other person on our church staff. I've just been called and divinely placed in this position by God. Just as our staff would be wrong not to be submissive, wives, you would be wrong to rebel and oppose God's order in the marriage even when you may be superior to your husband in some areas.

3) Man's Part

The apostle Paul instructed married men,

"Husbands, love your wives, just as Christ also loved the church and gave Himself for her" (Eph. 5:25).

The wife is called upon to love her husband enough to live for him. The husband is called upon to love his wife enough to die for her.

Watch out for the man who is always putting his wife down. A man is to love and protect his wife while at the same time treating her as his most prized treasure.

Today we have a lot of men who are just jerks - that's Greek for "lousy husband."

Christ intercedes for His bride, the church. He constantly watches over her and intercedes for her. Husbands are to continually watch over their bride, lifting her up, believing in her, loving her.

Jesus said, "I will build My church (bride), and the gates of Hades shall not prevail against it (her)" (Matt. 16:18). A husband should say, "I will love, protect, and provide for my bride and not let the pressures of this world come against her."

Marriage is not a 50-50 proposition; it is a 100-100-100 proposition.

Why are marriage promises being broken?

3. We have forgotten the consequences.

Through the prophet Jeremiah, God said to Israel,

> "They say, 'If a man divorces his wife, And she goes from him And becomes another man's, May he return to her again?' Would not that land be greatly polluted? But you have played the harlot with many lovers; Yet return to Me,' says the LORD . . . 'you have polluted the land with your harlotries and your wickedness . . . You have had a harlot's forehead; You refuse to be ashamed'" (Jer. 3:1-3).

Sounds like the Jerry Springer Show. Like Israel, we have become a nation that no longer knows how to blush or to be embarrassed.

The consequences of a failed marriage can be never ending. Judith Wallerstein writes in her book, *Second Chances: Men, Women and Children a Decade After Divorce*, "Divorce is deceptive. Legally it is a simple event, but psychologically it is a chain - sometimes a never-ending chain - of events, relocations and radically shifting relationships strung through time."

What are the consequences of divorce?

There is a lot of talk about divorce today (i.e., talk shows, magazines, etc.); however, we hear very little about the consequences of divorce. It reminds me of alcohol consumption in our country. Everything is made to look so good as we are bombarded with advertising. There was once a billboard with a smashed car pictured. The words read, "If you drink and drive, be prepared to live with your choices."

If you choose to drive down the highway of marriage and not do so according to God's laws, you are headed for a crash. When you marry outside of God's will, when you ignore God's Word and principles in your marriage, the consequences usually look like this: separation, divorce, an absentee parent, other relationships and marriages, other children, economic distress, and, usually, no male role model in the home.

If you make a choice to have an extramarital affair, be prepared to live with the consequences of it. The problem with our society is that we want the freedom to make choices, but we don't want to live with the consequences that are a result of our choices. Even being a Christian does not mean that you will not have to live with the consequences of your choices. David had to live with the consequences of his relationship with Bathsheba.

Why are marriage promises being broken?

4. We have forgotten Christ.

There are as many Christians getting divorces today as non-Christians. That should break your heart. There's not a distinguishable difference between Christians and non-Christians in divorce statistics. Yet the Bible says, *"For you will be His witness to all men of what you have seen and heard"* (Acts 22:15).

Just think about it. We are making a statement to the world that being a Christian doesn't make a difference. We are saying that knowing Jesus, going to church, reading your Bible, and praying don't make any difference in our marriage. We preach that God is powerful. Yet when our marriage breaks up we are communicating that God cannot fix the problem. When a Christian couple goes through a divorce, we communicate that Jesus can calm the seas, heal the sick, cast out demons, and raise the dead, but He can do nothing for my marriage.

The divorce of a Christian couple dishonors the Lord! By the way, the Bible never suggests that if you are not married you are in danger of missing out on God's best. The Bible makes it clear that God's best for us is a relationship with Him.

The church that focuses more on getting people married off than on getting people right with God is a church that actually feeds our society's divorce rates. The church should provide sound biblical teaching on what makes great marriages and what makes lousy ones. Let's help those who are already married and those who will be married at a future date.

Why are marriage promises being broken?

5. We have forgotten the cost.

We have forgotten the cost of immorality and divorce. Solomon reminds us of the cost of loose morals.

> "With her enticing speech she caused him to yield, With her flattering lips she seduced him. Immediately he went after her, as an ox goes to the slaughter, Or as a fool to the correction of the stocks, Till an arrow struck his liver. As a bird hastens to the snare, He did not know it would cost his life" (Prov. 7:21-23).

Let me mention four different costs of divorce:

A. Divorce increases the potential for failure.

There is a tendency that if we get a divorce we will also fail in other areas of our life. People who cannot keep their commitment in marriage cannot keep their commitment in other areas of their life. If they will get out of the marriage vows, they will break other vows also.

B. Divorce lowers the standard for your family.

When we lower the standard, it's easier for our children, brothers, and sisters to lower the standard. Our divorce opens the door for others to do likewise. About nine out of ten people who accept divorce and remarriage say that they accept it because someone in their family got a divorce.

There are three reasons why Dianne and I have been, and are still, committed to our marriage: our three daughters Jennifer, Jill, and Jaren. Now that we have seven grandchildren, Dianne and I have ten reasons to make our marriage work. We never want one of our daughters or grandchildren saying it's all right to divorce because of us. We must live this commitment out for our children and grandchildren to see and witness.

C. Divorce affects your funeral.

The death rate for divorced males is much higher than for men who are married. Divorce will unravel your life and create all kinds of stress for you. Johnny Carson once joked, "Married men live longer than single men. But married men are a lot more willing to die." Well, I hope you don't feel like that.

D. Divorce affects your finances.

There are four people involved in a divorce. The wife and her attorney, and the husband and his attorney. Two of the four win!

There is a tremendous economic impact regarding divorce. There is the cost of legal fees and of the divorce. Women and children usually experience a tremendous decline in their standard of living after a divorce, and there is the cost of alimony and child support.

Then, there is the cost of comparisons between the last mate and the present mate, comparisons between the last family and this family. If we don't fix our problems, we just carry our problems into the next marriage. Our job is not to FIND the right person; our job is to BE the right person.

If you are divorced, you cannot go back and make a brand new start, but you can start from here and make a brand new end. Don't focus on where you have been; focus on where you are going.

Before divorcing, let me offer these suggestions.

Considerations Before Divorce

1) Do I have God's approval to end this covenant?

Ask yourself, "Is this divorce scriptural? Do I have any biblical justification to stand on?"

2) Do I have the approval of my church?

Seek the biblical counsel of your pastor. *"Obey those who rule over you, and be submissive, for they watch out for your souls"* (Heb. 13:17). You should get godly counseling.

Many times a couple has already resolved to get a divorce, and as a last effort they go see the preacher and want him to perform a miracle. Folks, the miracle is when we commit to our marriage no matter what!

3) Do I have the approval of my conscience?

We have to live with ourselves and our choices.

4) Do I have the approval of other Christians?

What do people say who love God, who love me, and who know the Scripture?

Why are marriage promises being broken?

6. We have forgotten our children.

Solomon says,

"Children's children are the crown of old men, And the glory of children is their father" (Prov. 17:6).

Someone once said that, "No one should be given the right to have children unless they prove they have the ability to stay together."

Every day in America:
• Children see their parents divorce.
• Children are put into adult jails.
• Children run away from home.
• Children drop out of school.
• Teens become sexually active.

Just about every social problem imaginable is the result of destructive homes.

• About eight out of ten adolescents in psychiatric hospitals come from broken families.

• About three out of four teenage suicides come from homes where one parent is absent.

• A high percentage of teenage violent crimes and burglary comes from single-parent homes.

If the two-parent family cannot stay intact, the result on our society will be disastrous.

Divorce shatters stability in the minds of children. Divorce forces children to take sides. The American culture is a dangerous place for children today with abortion, abuse, sexual predators, liberal judges, and the breakup of marriages and homes. God help us!

I am asking you today to make a commitment to your marriage:

I am standing for the healing of my marriage! I won't give up, give in, give out, or give over till that healing takes place. I made a vow, I gave the pledge, I gave a ring, I took a ring, I gave myself, I trusted God. I said the words, and meant the words . . . "in sickness and in health, in sorrow and in joy, for better or for worse, for richer or for poorer, in good times and in bad," so I'm standing now, and won't sit down, let down, slow down, calm down, fall down, look down, or be down till the breakdown is torn down!

I refuse to put my eyes on outward circumstances, or listen to voices of doom, or buy into what's trendy, worldly, popular, convenient, easy, quick, thrifty, or advantageous. I will not settle for a cheap imitation of God's real thing, nor will I seek to lower God's standard, twist God's will, rewrite God's Word, violate God's covenant, or accept what God hates, namely divorce.

In a world of filth . . . I will stay pure. Surrounded by lies . . . I will speak the truth. Where hopelessness abounds . . . I will hope in God. Where revenge is easier . . . I will bless instead of curse. And where the odds are stacked against me . . . I'll trust God's faithfulness.

I'm a stander, and I won't compromise, quarrel, or quit. I have made the choice, set my face, entered the race, believed the Word, and trusted God for all the outcome.

I will allow neither the reaction of my spouse, nor the urging of my friends, nor the advice of my loved ones, nor the economic hardship, nor the prompting of the devil to make me let up, slow up, blow up, or give up till my marriage is healed up.

The First Marriage

The garden of Eden provided a beautiful setting for the first wedding.

> And the LORD God said, "It is not good that man should be alone; I will make him a helper comparable to him." Out of the ground the LORD God formed every beast of the field and every bird of the air, and brought them to Adam to see what he would call them. And whatever Adam called each living creature, that was its name. So Adam gave names to all cattle, to the birds of the air, and to every beast of the field. But for Adam there was not found a helper comparable to him. And the LORD God caused a deep sleep to fall on Adam, and he slept; and He took one of his ribs, and closed up the flesh in its place. Then the rib which the LORD God had taken from man He made into a woman, and He brought her to the man. And Adam said: "This is now bone of my bones and flesh of my flesh; She shall be called Woman, because she was taken out of Man." Therefore a man shall leave his father and mother and be joined to his wife, and they shall become one flesh. And they were both naked, the man and his wife, and were not ashamed (Genesis 2:18-25).

Someone has suggested that those who translated the original manuscripts of the Bible into English overlooked and omitted a few verses that go something like this.

God asked Adam, "What is wrong with you?" Adam said, "Lord, I don't have anyone to talk to or to share my life with." So God told Adam that He was going to make for him a companion, and that it would be a woman. God told Adam, "She will gather food for you, cook for you, and when you discover clothing she'll wash it for you. She will always agree with every decision you make. She will bear you children and never ask you to get up in the middle of the night to take care of them. She will not nag you and will always be the first to admit she was wrong when you've had a disagreement. She will never have a headache and will freely and frequently give her love to you."

Adam asked God, "What will a woman like this cost me?" God answered Adam and said, "An arm and a leg." Then Adam asked, "What can I get for a rib?" And the rest is history.

Of course, that's not exactly how the story of the first marriage goes.

A little boy once asked his father, "Daddy, how much does it cost to get married?" The father replied, "I don't know son, I'm still paying."

After creating for six days, God looked at all He had made and, *"indeed it was very good"* (Gen. 1:31). But before God gave us the first marriage, He saw something that was "not good" (Gen. 2:18). The man He had created was alone. Why was this not good? After all, Adam could fellowship with God, enjoy the beauty and the food of the garden, and even play with and rule over the animals.

All of God's creation was complete. Yet when God created a man, he was incomplete without a woman. God knew that Adam needed a companion. Therefore, God said He would *"make him a helper."* God must have known that man needed help.

If ever there was a perfect marriage, we see it here. This was a perfect marriage because of two reasons:

1. It was a perfect wedding because of what Adam and Eve had. They had the perfect wedding place. The wedding took place in the most picturesque setting imaginable--the garden of Eden. A garden that God Himself planted (Gen. 2:8). The flowers were unbelievably beautiful. The food for the reception came right out of the garden. It

was a perfect wedding because of who the Wedding Director was - God Himself.

2. It was a perfect wedding because of what Adam and Eve didn't have. It was a perfect wedding because it was void of any sin. And it was a perfect wedding because neither the bride nor groom inherited in-laws. This was indeed a perfect wedding.

It has been suggested that a perfect wedding today would be the marriage of a deaf man to a blind woman.

Let us consider two things about the first marriage:

1. The beginning of marriage

We see the beginning of marriage, the first marriage, which was instigated and instituted by God.

Notice these three things in Genesis 2 about the beginning of marriage:

A. Our need is foreknown by God.

When did Adam realize that he was lonely? When did Adam realize he had no helper or companion? Not until verse 20, *But for Adam there was not found a helper comparable to him.*

When did God know that Adam was incomplete without a mate? In verse 18, God said, *"It is not good that man should be alone; I will make him a helper comparable to him."* Long before Adam knew of his need, God already knew. God anticipated Adam's need. Eve was in the mind and heart of God long before she was in the arms of Adam.

God did the same thing for all of us in regard to our need for salvation. That is why Jesus is *"the Lamb slain from the foundation of the world"* (Rev. 13:8). You see, salvation was in the heart of God before sin was in the heart of man.

God knew exactly what Adam needed even before Adam knew. God knows what you and I need as well. We often get into trouble and create a mess when we run ahead of God and try to meet our own needs outside of His will. If you think you need a mate, why don't you take that to the Lord? He knows your heart, He knows your need, and He will meet those needs in His will. The real issue is not, "Can God meet my need?" The issue is, "Can I trust God to bring into my life the one He has made just for me?"

God knows better than you who you should marry.

B. Our need is fostered by God.

We notice how God nurtures and encourages this relationship between Adam and Eve. God brought all the animals that He had created to Adam, and Adam gave to each creature a name. It became very obvious to Adam that every animal had a mate, that there was a male and a female. This must have aroused and stirred up Adam's awareness that he had no mate, no *"helper comparable to him"* (vs. 18, 20).

God never stirs up a desire that He cannot satisfy. If you do not have the gift of celibacy and God puts it in your heart to marry, He can satisfy you with a mate. The problem is that in our sex-induced society we allow the world, and not God, to stir us up. Our passions are often aroused long before their time, making it difficult to wait on the Lord and His will.

God has a way of fostering relationships. I believe He fostered my relationship with Dianne. During her senior year in high school, Dianne worked a part-time job at a Sears and Roebuck Store. A girl named Rhonda, who attended my high school, worked with her and introduced us. We went out on our first date with Rhonda and her boyfriend, after which Dianne spent the night with her. Dianne's father let her spend the night with Rhonda only if they went to church the next morning. Well, Rhonda didn't go to church regularly, so the next morning I was surprised when I got to church there was Dianne. That impressed me because I knew I needed to marry a Christian girl who loved the Lord and loved the church. My need for the right kind of wife was being fostered.

C. Our need is fulfilled by God.

God fulfilled Adam's need with the creation of Eve. Adam needed Eve. No animal could do for Adam what Eve could.

Now Eve was not inferior to Adam in any way. Both were made in the image of God. *So God created man in His own image; in the image of God He created him; male and female He created them* (Genesis 1:27).

God didn't make males and males, or females and females. God created them *"male and female."* God made us different, and I like the difference.

Did you hear about the wife who walked into the kitchen and found her husband walking around with a fly swatter. She asked him, "What are you doing?" He replied, "I'm hunting flies." She said, "Are you killing any?" To which he replied, "I've already killed three males and two females." Intrigued, the wife said, "How can you tell the difference between a male fly and a female fly?" He responded, "Easily, three flies were on the meatloaf, and two flies were on the telephone."

The word *"man"* used here in Genesis 1:27 is the Hebrew word "adam" and it means "a human being." Both male and female were created in the image of God. And both of them were to have dominion over the earth (Gen. 1:29).

Notice what Adam did while God was creating Eve: he slept, giving us the picture that he was resting in the Lord. This is exactly what many single people need to do while waiting on the Lord to give them a mate. They need to rest in the Lord, casting all their care upon Him.

Eve was not made out of Adam's head to rule over him (woman is not superior to man), nor out of his feet to be trampled on by him (woman is not inferior to man), but out of his side to be equal with him, under his arm to be protected by him, and near his heart to be dear to him.

The word *"rib"* (Gen. 2:21 & 22), means "a side." God took a side of Adam and formed Eve. A side would include bone, flesh, and blood. After Eve was presented to Adam, he would say, *"This is now bone of my bones and flesh of my flesh; she shall be called Woman, because she was taken out of Man"* (vs. 23). From the life of Adam, God made him a bride and presented her to him.

In the New Testament we see another "side" which produced a bride. On the cross they pierced the side of Jesus and *"blood and water came out"* (Jn. 19:34). From the life of Jesus, God made Him a bride and will one day present her to Him.

Marriage is honorable, but this was surely the most honorable of all marriages, for Adam and Eve knew no sin and God's hand was in every detail of their marriage. We like to say, "This was a marriage made in heaven." Well, Adam and Eve could certainly say this and be accurate.

God made them both; now He makes them one. God, as Eve's Father, brought her to Adam. And God, as Adam's Father, gave him a wife.

> *God made them both; now He makes them one.*

I believe it is necessary that children from Christian homes should have their parents' consent and blessing to marry.

2. The benefit of marriage

Marriage is God's idea for the blessing and benefit of mankind. No matter what the world says, what the talk shows say, or what the courts say, God had the first word on marriage. And, He will have the last word on marriage. *Marriage is honorable among all, and the bed undefiled; but fornicators and adulterers God will judge* (Heb. 13:4).

When God does something for us, it always benefits us. In creation God gave to us the institution of marriage, the bringing together of man and woman. On the cross God gave to us salvation, the bringing together of the bride and the Bridegroom.

Let me mention four benefits of marriage:

A. Marriage provides a partnership.

In marriage, God gives to us companionship. When God said, *"It is not good that man should be alone"* (vs. 18), He did not mean that this was evil, but rather that a man alone was unfinished and therefore imperfect.

Statistically a single-parent home is very disadvantaged compared to a home with both parents. Today's unholy culture is a reflection of unhealthy families. We have believed a lie that the traditional family is irrelevant, and the two-parent home isn't necessary.

B. Marriage provides for procreation.

Marriage gives to us the God-given right to enjoy a physical relationship and to reproduce children. As a matter of fact, God said to them, *"Be fruitful and multiply"* (Gen. 1:28).

This first marriage was consummated as Adam and Eve became *"one flesh"* as they complemented each other physically, mentally, and spiritually. *And they were both naked, the man and his wife, and were not ashamed* (vs. 25). Adam and Eve were naked yet they were not ashamed.

Why do you think they were not ashamed? They were alone. There were no other people around. Their physiological differences had been divinely created by God and according to His purposes, so they were perfectly natural with each other. They were still innocent, with no consciousness of sin or guilt.

They could not obey the command of God to "Be fruitful and multiply," without using the bodies that He gave them. Later, after sin, they realized their nakedness and covered their reproductive parts. But in the beginning there was no shame because there was no sin.

Without a doubt, one of the primary uses of the physical union was for procreation, to "Be fruitful and multiply." Now some believe that procreation is the only reason for the physical union. However, the apostle Paul gives us another reason when he said, "It is better to marry than to burn with passion" (1 Cor. 7:9).

That brings us to the third benefit of marriage.

C. Marriage provides for purity.

Marriage encourages our purity and self-control. In a marriage *"The wife does not have authority over her own body, but the husband does. And likewise the husband does not have authority over his own body, but the wife does."* (1 Cor. 7:4).

God honors sexual desire and sexual expression within a marriage. For husbands and wives to deny each other sexually dishonors God because it dishonors marriage which God instituted and ordained. Sexual expression within a marriage is not an option. Paul commands married couples, *"Do not deprive one another"* (1 Cor. 7:5).

On the other hand, you show me a marriage that is built solely on a physical relationship and I will show you a marriage that is weak and immature.

D. Marriage provides a picture.

The marriage between a man and a woman gives us many beautiful pictures of Jesus (the Bridegroom) and believers (the bride).

1. In a Jewish wedding, the bridegroom took the initiative and traveled from his father's house to the home of the bride.

Jesus left heaven, His Father's house, and came to earth to take the initiative to gain a bride.

2. The father of the prospective bride would negotiate with the prospective bridegroom a price that must be paid to purchase his bride.

On the cross Jesus paid the price of His own blood to gain a bride.

3. When the bridegroom made a commitment and paid the purchase price, the marriage covenant was validated. This was called the betrothal period. The man and woman were then considered husband and wife, even though the union had not yet been consummated.

When one commits his life to Christ, he is sanctified, or set apart, to belong solely to Jesus Christ.

4. When the wedding covenant was established the bridegroom and bride drank from a cup symbolizing the relationship had been established.

On the Thursday night before His crucifixion, Jesus established the Lord's Supper symbolizing our relationship with Him had been established.

5. After the marriage covenant had been established, the bridegroom went back to his father's house and remained separated from his bride for a period of twelve months.

After Jesus paid the price for His bride and established the marriage covenant, He ascended back to heaven, His Father's house, where He waits until He returns for His bride.

6. During this betrothal period of separation, the bride prepared herself for marriage. The bridegroom, in the meantime, prepared living accommodations for his bride.

Today the Lord has sent pastors and teachers to prepare the bride of Christ. All the while, Jesus is preparing a place for us. Jesus said, *"I go to prepare a place for you. And if I go and prepare a place for you, I will come again and receive you to Myself; that where I am, there you may be also"* (Jn. 14:2-3).

7. After the betrothal period the bridegroom, along with the wedding party, came at night with torchlights to get the bride.

One day Jesus will come to get the bride. *"For the Lord Himself with descend from heaven with a shout, with the voice of an archangel, and with the trumpet of God . . . Then we . . . shall be caught up together with them in the clouds to meet the Lord in the air. And thus we shall always be with the Lord"* (1 Thess. 4:16-17).

8. The bride was expecting her groom to come for her, but she did not know the exact time. So, the bridegroom's arrival was preceded by a shout.

As believers, we expect Jesus' return, but we do not know when. His return will be preceded by a shout.

9. The groom carried his bride to her new, permanent home and in the privacy of that place, they consummated the marriage.

When Jesus comes, He will take us to our new, permanent home, and there we will enjoy His fellowship and presence, beginning at the marriage supper of the Lamb and continuing throughout eternity.

What Happens After I Say "I Do"?

God established in the Garden the first marriage (Gen. 2:18-25), yet God said nothing about divorce. After Adam and Eve said "I do," and by the time of Moses, difficulty had developed in many marriages. Moses instructed the people,

"When a man takes a wife and marries her, and it happens that she finds no favor in his eyes because he has found some uncleanness in her, and he writes her a certificate of divorce, puts it in her hand, and sends her out of his house, when she has departed from his house, and goes and becomes another man's wife, if the latter husband detests her and writes her a certificate of divorce, puts it in her hand, and sends her out of his house, or if the latter husband dies who took her as his wife, then her former husband who divorced her must not take her back to be his wife after she has been defiled; for that is an abomination before the LORD, and you shall not bring sin on the land which the LORD your God is giving you as an inheritance" (Deut. 24:1-4).

Jesus would later say, "Moses, because of the hardness of your hearts, permitted you to divorce your wives, but from the beginning it was not so" (Matt. 19:8). Jesus goes on to say, ". . . whoever divorces his wife, except for sexual immorality, and marries another, commits adultery; and whoever marries her who is divorced commits adultery" (Matt. 19:9).

Marriage is primarily a physical relationship. Paul said, *"It is better to marry than to burn"* (1 Cor. 7:9). Paul was speaking about the physical. Therefore, when the physical relationship was broken, either by death or adultery, the innocent spouse was free to remarry. However, in the case of adultery, divorce was a concession for the innocent party, not a command to the innocent party.

Jesus permitted divorce because of sexual immorality and in doing so was equating divorce with death. In the Old Testament the law required an adulterer to be put to death. Today in the New Testament church we don't kill people for adultery, homosexuality, or any other sin. But we can accept divorce as a result of sexual sin as the equivalent of death, therefore conceding to the innocent spouse the right to remarry.

Let me be clear. It is my conviction after studying Scripture, that you can be remarried if the basis for your divorce is adultery and you are the innocent party.

> *In the case of adultery, divorce was a concession for the innocent party, not a command to the innocent party.*

I'm often asked this question, "My spouse divorced me with no scriptural grounds. Am I free to remarry?" The answer is "No, not until your spouse is sexually joined with another." Up to this point your marriage has not been broken physically; therefore, in the eyes of God you are still married. And if you remarry, you cut off the Holy Spirit's working in both of your lives to reconcile the marriage.

What Happens After I Say "I Do"?

After Marriage . . .

1. Most of us want to make our marriage work.

When the wedding bells ring, when we say those wedding vows, none of us do so with the expectation of failure. All us want to make our marriage work.

2. All of us have to work on our marriage.

A marriage doesn't work on its on. If you have been married for two hours, you already know it is going to take a lot of work.

3. Many marriages don't work.

In many of today's marriages the wedding vows have been changed from "Until death do we part," to "For as long as we continue to love each other," or "For as long as our love shall last," or "Until our time together is over."

The divorce of movie stars Brad Pitt and Jennifer Aniston has been much publicized. Brad Pitt said he didn't consider his marriage to Jennifer Aniston a failure but rather called it a total success. He goes on to say that he was with her five years longer than he's been with anyone else.

4. Many of us don't know how to work on our marriage.

Many people do not know how to relate in a marriage because they had poor models. They were the product of a broken home where they had no example of two people working on their marriage.

Out of the four reasons above, did you notice one word that was common to them all? Work! The marriage usually works well through the honeymoon, but after that we realize that we have to work at our marriage.

What happens after you say "I do"? Let me mention four things that affect marriage:

1. The calculation of marriage

What are your expectations of marriage?

Each marriage partner has grown up differently, had different experiences, and therefore can carry into the marriage a set of expectations different from the one they are marrying.

My wife, Dianne, and I grew up differently and entered the marriage with our own calculations of what we thought our marriage would be like and what roles we would fulfill. I grew up in a single-parent home. Everything that was done at our house my mom did. So I entered into marriage expecting Dianne to do everything in the home. I thought all I had to do was to work hard to earn a pay check, then come home to a hot supper, the newspaper, and a bowl of ice cream before bedtime. The rest I calculated that Dianne would take care of. Wrong! Dianne grew up in a home with a healthy marriage relationship where her mom and dad helped each other. I remember one of the first times I had a meal with her family. After we ate, her father helped her mother with the dirty dishes. I could hardly believe my eyes. I thought doing dishes was something only a woman would do. Wrong! Dianne expected me to help her around the house. After all, she grew up watching her mom and dad working together.

Marriages break up for many reasons. Let me mention three:

1. We RUSH into marriage.

We think we can't wait, and so we don't.

2. We RELY on divorce as a way out.

We enter into marriage knowing that if it gets too hot, divorce is our fire escape.

An engaged couple was filling out their marriage certificate. One of the questions asked was, "Which marriage is this?" The groom put down "First." The bride put down "Last."

3. We confuse love with ROMANCE.

Now there is nothing wrong with romance, but it is not the same as love. Let me mention a few differences between romance and love:

Romance is departing . . . Love is devoting.

Romance seeks perfection . . . Love forgives imperfection.

Romance demands observation . . . Love gives consideration.

Romance is exciting . . . Love is endearing.

Romance is going somewhere . . . Love is being there.

Romance is always striving to be attractive . . . Love is two people who find beauty in each other no matter how they look.

Romance is the anguish of waiting for the phone to ring so someone can give you words of affection . . . Love is the anguish of waiting for the phone to ring so someone can give you words of assurance (they are happy and safe).

Romance is dancing in the moonlight and gazing into the eyes of someone across a candlelit table . . . Love is saying, "I'll get up this time, Honey," and you stumble in the dark to warm a baby's bottle or comfort a frightened child.

Romance is delicious . . . Love is nourishing.

Romance can't last . . . Love can.

That's good stuff!

2. The concentration of marriage

Before marriage we concentrate on our mate; after marriage we concentrate on ourselves!

Here's a word of advice: If you're dating someone who is selfish, you ain't seen nothing yet! Wait till you're married!

If you're dating someone who is selfish, you ain't seen nothing yet! Wait till you're married!

The following poem illustrates how our focus shifts after we are married.

> ***Two lovers walking down the street,***
> ***She trips, he murmurs, "Careful sweet."***
> ***Now wed they trend the same street,***
> ***She trips, he growls, "Pick up your feet."***

This shift of *concentration* is seen very vividly as we observe the difference between premarital counseling and postmartial counseling.

Premarital counseling goes something like this: The couple comes to the church to visit the pastor for premarital counseling. As they drive into the church parking lot they are sitting almost on top of each other (you're not sure if there's one or two people in the car). He opens her door and helps her out of the car. They walk into the office arm-in-arm. They sit in the office and gaze into each other eyes. The pastor, trying to get their attention, has to say, "Hey, I'm over here. Remember me, you came in to see me."

The pastor asks them several questions:

Pastor, "How long have you known each other?"

Couple, "Three months."

Pastor, "Do you have a job?"

Couple, "No."

Pastor, "Are you going to get a job?"

Couple, "After the honeymoon."

Pastor, "Do you have a car?"

Couple, "Well, we use our friend's car when he's not using it."

The whole time the pastor's talking to them they don't look at him; they have goo-goo eyes for each other. When they leave, the pastor thinks he's just wasted an hour because they didn't hear a word he said.

In premarital counseling they are so in love that they never see any problems. They don't see any weaknesses in each other.

Postmarital counseling goes something like this: The same couple comes to see the pastor two years later. They squeal into the parking lot. He gets out of the car on his side; she gets out on her side without any assistance from him. They both slam their car door and walk angrily toward the office door. They come into the office and sit on opposite sides of the room. The gazing look they used to have, has turned into a glaring look.

Now they both have jobs and a car. The things they didn't have before the marriage, but said they could make it, they now have but say they can't make it.

The reason they can't make it is because before marriage they couldn't see any wrong in each other. They saw each other through the very best eyes. After marriage they glare at each other and can easily find weaknesses in their mate.

She thinks everything is his fault. He thinks everything is her fault. The problem is that before they were married they looked at each other from an "other perspective." Now that they are married, they look at things from a "me perspective." Before marriage we focus on our mate. After marriage our focus shifts to ourself.

At our marriage we say "I do." After our marriage we say, "I don't." Before marriage we would run miles out of the way to do her a favor. After marriage, we don't

> *At our marriage we say "I do." After our marriage we say, "I don't."*

even want to stop on the way home from work for a gallon of milk.

If you will work as hard after you're married as you did before you were married, your marriage can make it.

Dating brings out the best; marriage brings out the rest.

3. The cleaving of marriage

During the creation account, Scripture informs us that "a man shall leave his father and mother and be joined (KJV uses the word "cleave") to his wife, and they shall become one flesh" (Gen. 2:24). Jesus would later quote this verse in Matthew 19:5. The word "cleave" used here means "to fasten, to cling, to adhere, to glue, or to join." We find here . . .

The Principles of Cleaving

1) Evacuation

The word "leave" here means "to loosen, to relinquish, to forsake, or leave behind, to abandon." When you get married, you're no longer a part of your mom and dad's family; you and your spouse are your own family now.

2) Consecration

A man and woman in marriage are set apart for one another. *"A man shall leave his father and mother and be joined to his wife"* (Gen. 2:24). This joining of husband and wife is to be permanent. They are to be glued together, and it is God's desire and design that they not become unglued.

3) Unification

"They shall become one flesh." To be *"one flesh"* once again emphasizes that marriage is primarily a physical relationship. To be *"one flesh"* means that you belong completely and entirely to one another.

The marriage relationship also affects our spiritual being. Let me tell you what I often see: husbands, as leaders of their home, who restrict the spiritual growth of their wife and children. Ladies, one of your main concerns in looking for a marriage partner is to find someone who can lead you spiritually. A husband who will encourage, and not restrict, your spiritual growth.

The temperature in your home is determined by a thermostat located somewhere in the house. If the air temperature is too cold or too hot, we adjust the thermostat. Men, you are the spiritual thermostat in your home. If the spiritual temperature in your home and with your wife and kids is not like it should be, you need some spiritual adjustment.

4) Cohabitation

"And they were both naked." This speaks of intimacy. No one should know you like your spouse does.

4. The contrast of marriage

Have you ever noticed that men and women are different? God made us *"male"* and *"female"* (Gen. 1:27).

We make a big mistake in our marriage when we think that our spouse's needs are the same as ours. No way, Jose!

Did you hear about the man who was walking along the beach in California one day when he stumbled across a bottle. He picked it up, opened it, and out popped a genie. The genie thanked the man and told the man that he had been in that bottle for thousands of years. The genie then granted the man a wish. The man thought for a moment. He had always wanted to go to Hawaii but was afraid to fly or travel by boat. Therefore, the man said to the genie, "I want you to build a highway from the California coast to Hawaii." The genie thought for a moment and said, "That would be too difficult. Do you have another request?" The man said, "Could you help me understand women? Help me understand what makes them tick?" The genie thought for a moment and replied, "Did you want a two- or four-lane highway?"

In his book, *His Needs, Her Needs* Dr. Willard Harley, Jr. identifies the needs of both the man and the woman.

He says that man's five most basic needs in marriage are:

1) Sexual fulfillment
2) Recreational companionship
3) An attractive spouse
4) Domestic support
5) Admiration

Do you think any of man's five basic needs show up on the woman's list? No!

The woman's five most basic needs in marriage are:

1) Affection
2) Conversation

Women generally need more communication than men do.

Two women were talking one day; let's follow their conversation:

Woman 1: "Oh! You got a haircut, it's soooo cute!"

Woman 2: "Do you think so? I wasn't sure when she gave me the mirror. I mean, you don't think it's too fluffy looking, do you?"

Woman 1: "Oh honey, it's perfect! I'd love to get my hair cut like that, but I think my face is too wide. I'm pretty much stuck with this stuff, I think."

Woman 2: "Are you serious? I think your face is adorable! And you could easily get one of those layer cuts. That would look so cute, I think. I was actually going to do that except that I was afraid it would accent my long neck."

Woman 1: "Oh, that's funny! I would love to have your neck. Anything to take away this blocked shoulder line of mine."

Woman 2: "Are you kidding? I know girls that would love to have your shoulders. Everything drapes so well on you. I mean, look at my arms, they are so short. If I had your shoulders, I could get clothes to fit me so much easier."

Man's version of this story goes like this:

Man 1: "Haircut?"

Man 2: "Yep."

Women want to talk; men want the bottom line.

Before marriage a man will lie awake thinking about something his fiance said. After marriage he will fall asleep before his wife can say it.

3) Honesty and openness

4) Financial support

It's been said that a woman worries about the future until she gets a husband. A man never worries about the future until he gets a wife.

5) Family commitment

A man can have the best intentions to meet his wife's needs, but if he thinks her needs are similar to his own, he will fail miserably. And when women assume men appreciate the same things they do, they will fail.

You know what you get out of marriage? Usually what you're looking for. A man went to church and left disappointed. He said, "The temperature was too hot, the organist played some wrong notes, and the preacher used poor grammar." Another man went to church and left encouraged and uplifted saying, "The music stirred my soul. God used the pastor's message speak to my heart, and I felt I was in the presence of God." He left church saying, "It was good to be in the house of the Lord." The moral of the story: Both men went to the same church, and both got what they were looking for.

Your marriage can work and can be greatly enjoyed, but it depends on what you are looking for.

Let me close this chapter by encouraging you to pray for your spouse.

A Prayer for Married Ladies

"Dear Lord, I want to thank you for my husband and the way You use him to bless me and to mold Your character in my life. Help me to be a godly wife who loves as You love and forgives as You forgive. I ask Your forgiveness, dear Lord, for the times when I have been unkind, impatient, and unforgiving.

"I pray for a hedge of protection around my husband and our marriage. I pray that my primary attraction, affection, and attention is reserved for my husband alone. Dear Lord, continue teaching me how to create an atmosphere in our home that reflects Your love for us and our love for You.

"I ask You to bless my husband as together we strive to set the example in our home and neighborhood of what a Christian home should be. I, too, commit myself afresh and anew, first to You, dear Lord, and then to my husband. In Jesus' Name. Amen."

A Prayer for Married Men

"Dear Lord Jesus, thank You for the wife You have given me. Fill me daily with Your Holy Spirit so that I may love her the same as You have loved me. Forgive me for those times when I have taken her for granted. I ask Your forgiveness, Lord, for the many times when I have failed as the spiritual leader of our marriage and home. I recommit this day to my responsibility of taking the initiative and setting the example of being the loving, spiritual leader of our marriage and home.

"I ask for Your wisdom in reordering the spiritual priorities of our home. I also ask for Your hedge of protection around our marriage so that my primary attraction, affection, and attention is reserved for my wife alone. I confess my own inabilities to be the role model set forth in Your Word. So I humbly ask You now to fill me with Your Holy Spirit in order for the love of Jesus to find expression through my life. I commit myself afresh and anew, first to You, dear Lord, and then to my wife. In Jesus' Name. Amen."

Is There a
Hex on Sex?

Is sex evil? People generally view sex in one of two ways, which are both wrong:

1. We view sex as DEMONIC.

Even in the church we usually view sex as something dirty instead of something delightful. When is the last time you heard something positive said about sex at church?

Yet God created sex and gave it to us. Just as we need to have a Christian world view, we need to develop a Christian view on sex, because God created sex. If you want the right perspective on sex don't pick up a Playboy magazine, pick up your Bible. The Bible tells it like it is and is a must read on the subject.

Sex is not evil; it is the misuse of sex that is evil. Too often we blame Satan for sex instead of thanking God for the blessing of sex.

A second way in which people wrongly view sex is:

2. We view sex as a DEITY.

Sex has become the god that we worship. How else do you explain the popularity and celebrity status of Jerry Springer and Howard Stern? Adult entertainment is one of America's fastest growing industries. The popularity of pornography is evident by the emphasis and attention it receives from millions of people.

Instead of looking to the cybersmut on various web sites about sex, let us look to the Bible to find out about sex. Instead of reading what

Hugh Hefner or Larry Flint have to say on the subject, let us read what the apostle Paul has to say about the subject.

> Now concerning the things of which you wrote to me: It is good for a man not to touch a woman. Nevertheless, because of sexual immorality, let each man have his own wife, and let each woman have her own husband. Let the husband render to his wife the affection due her, and likewise also the wife to her husband. The wife does not have authority over her own body, but the husband does. And likewise the husband does not have authority over his own body, but the wife does. Do not deprive one another except with consent for a time, that you may give yourselves to fasting and prayer; and come together again so that Satan does not tempt you because of your lack of self-control. But I say this as a concession, not as a commandment (1 Corinthians 7:1-6).

Let us consider four things regarding sex, singleness, and marriage:

1. The celibacy of the single person

Evidently the Corinthians were having difficulty regarding many of the same issues we deal with today - the matter of marriage and sex. Like that of today, much of their marital problems reflected the values of a morally bankrupt society. So they wrote to get the advice of the apostle Paul. We commend them that they sought godly counsel about this issue. The most important decision we will ever make is to accept Jesus Christ. After that the decision with regard to marriage is extremely important.

Paul said to them, *"Now concerning the things of which you wrote to me: It is good for a man not to touch a woman"* (vs. 1).

Here Paul is actually encouraging a celibate life style. Paul is not stating that marriage is inferior to being single; he is saying that being single is a good thing as long as one is celibate.

There are some today who would have us believe that the only purpose for sex is for procreation, since God created both male and female and told them, *"Be fruitful and multiply"* (Gen. 1:28). Therefore, the only reason for sex is to produce offspring because God commanded this. That brings about this problem: Does this mean that it is God's will for every person to marry and to produce offspring? Certainly Paul, inspired by the Holy Spirit, would not come along and encourage people to be celibate after God told us to *"Be fruitful and multiply."* Is Paul going against the command of God here? Certainly not. Paul was saying that it was *"good for a man not to touch a woman."* However, Paul would later say, *"It is better to marry than to burn with passion"* (1 Cor. 7:9), giving us yet another reason for marriage and sex- -to satisfy the desires of the flesh.

Paul acknowledges that being single is a good and honorable state, but he does not support the claim that it is a more spiritual state.

2. *The concern of the single person*

In verse 2 Paul offers some common sense in his advice to the Corinthians, *"Nevertheless, because of sexual immorality, let each man have his own wife, and let each woman have her own husband."* Paul is speaking to those who are single about the danger of sexual sin. When sexual desire is strong and temptation is great, Paul advises marriage.

Marriage is not only honorable, it is necessary. Through marriage the human race continues, the well-being of children is enhanced, and the desires of the flesh are met.

I would greatly encourage marriage, especially today, not because it is superior to being single, but because of the sex-inflamed society in which we live where everything is acceptable and available. While the Bible tells us that true love waits, our society believes, contrary to Scripture, that true love wears a condom.

Paul makes it abundantly clear that God approves of neither polygamy nor homosexuality. Paul says, *"Let each man have his own wife, and let each woman have her own husband."*

Now Paul is not suggesting that a Christian should go out and find another Christian to marry only for the purpose of relieving the flesh. Obviously there are other worthy considerations regarding marriage-- some of which Paul addresses in Ephesians 5 - but we must beware of sexual desire and temptation.

The Path to Sexual Sin

My son, keep your father's command, and do not forsake the law of your mother. Bind them continually upon your heart; tie them around your neck. When you roam, they will lead you; when you sleep, they will keep you; and when you awake, they will speak with you. For the commandment is a lamp, and the law a light; reproofs of instruction are the way of life, to keep you from the evil woman, from the flattering tongue of a seductress. Do not lust after her beauty in your heart, nor let her allure you with her eyelids. For by means of a harlot a man is reduced to a crust of bread; and an adulteress will prey upon his precious life (Proverbs 6:20-26).

Solomon, the writer of this Proverb, gives us five steps to sexual sin:

1) Association

Solomon said to, *"keep . . . from the evil woman"* (Prov. 6:24). The first step to sexual sin is association. Be careful regarding those with whom you associate, and on what the foundation of your friendship is based.

Solomon is speaking here about the character of a certain kind of woman. He refers to an *"evil woman."* It is an evil woman who would encourage sexual immorality. Beware of her lure which is motivated by her lust.

Parents, you must be tough here. Do not allow your children to date non-Christians. If your children don't date non-Christians, they won't marry non-Christians. Every person they date becomes a potential marriage partner.

2) Conversation

Solomon speaks of *"the flattering tongue of a seductress,"* or wayward wife (Prov. 6:24). We are to be aware, first of all, of her character. Secondly, we are to be aware of her conversation. She will flatter you. She knows what to say to make you think you are the most desirable guy in the world.

The longer a fish looks at the lure and swims around the lure, the more likely he is to get hooked by the lure. Just as that fishing lure looks good to the fish, the seductress looks good to the man. Hanging around her and conversing with her leads to the third step.

3) Imagination

Solomon said, *"Do not lust after her beauty in your heart"* (Prov. 6:25). At this stage, your imagination starts to run wild. You begin to fantasize and think about what it would be like to be with her. Your imagination leads to the fourth step.

4) Flirtation

Solomon said not to *"let her allure you with her eyelids"* (Prov. 6:25). You lust in your heart; you flirt with your eyes.

If anyone knows about these things it is Solomon with all of his wives and concubines. Solomon is telling us that this kind of woman knows how to talk to you through her eyes. Solomon knows. He had been fooled many times.

The last step to sexual sin is:

5) Fornication

Solomon said "For by means of a harlot a man is reduced to a crust of bread" (Prov. 6:26). Sexual immorality is devastating. It will leave an indelible mark on your soul, your mind, and your conscience. It will cost you self-respect, and it is a sin against God!

3. The command to the married couple

Paul commands the married couple,

> "Let the husband render to his wife the affection due her, and likewise also the wife to her husband. The wife does not have authority over her own body, but the husband does. And likewise the husband does not have authority over his own body, but the wife does" (vs. 3-4).

It is obvious that celibacy is wrong for those who are married. It is believed that some in the Corinthian church, including some who were married, thought it to be spiritually superior to refrain from sexual relations. In doing so, Paul said that they were neglecting and denying their responsibilities to their spouse.

You are not to withhold yourself from your spouse. The physical relationship between a husband and a wife is not only a privilege and a pleasure, it is a responsibility and an obligation.

Paul commands three things here:

A. The husband and wife should have a reciprocal relationship.

Paul says that both the husband and the wife should *"render . . . affection."* The King James Version says to *"render . . . due benevolence."* These words are interesting. The word *"render"* means *"to give away."* The word *"benevolence"* is used only this one time in the New Testament, and it refers to our conjugal duty. The physical relationship should be performed and experienced by both the husband and the wife in a mutual interchange.

If you are married it is your duty and obligation to meet the physical needs and desires of your spouse. If those needs are not legitimately satisfied, they might find satisfaction illegitimately.

B. The husband and wife should have a respectful relationship.

Paul said,

"The wife does not have authority (power or control) over her own body, but the husband does. And likewise the husband does not have authority (power or control) over his own body, but the wife does" (vs. 4).

Our bodies are controlled in three ways:

1. In the normal sense of living we are to take care of our bodies. We are to practice personal hygiene, we should eat properly and get some exercise. Our bodies are ours to take care of.

2. In a spiritual sense, our bodies belong to the Lord. Paul said that we are to *"present our bodies a living sacrifice, holy, acceptable to God"* (Rom. 12:1). As Christians, we have been bought with a price. We no longer belong to ourselves; we belong to Jesus. He has every right to demand from us the usage of our body, even if it means dying for Him as Stephen did.

3. In marriage our body no longer belongs to us but to our spouse. When either spouse is unreasonably demanding or unfairly frigid, it leads to resentment and trouble in the marriage.

In doing marriage counselling over the years, and in trying to understand the differences between men and women, I have observed that it is typical for the husband to have the stronger sex drive. Sex is much more physical for the man and much more emotional for the woman. When it comes to the physical relationship, the husband and wife can be on opposite ends of the spectrum. I suggest compromise. I suggest that a husband and wife respect each other. The husband needs to move closer to the wife's end of the spectrum, and the wife needs to move closer to the husband's end of the spectrum. Regardless of your personal preference, the needs of your spouse should be respected. There should be neither domination nor desertion in a marital relationship.

C. The husband and wife should not have a robbing relationship.

Paul commands husband and wife, *"Do not deprive one another"* (vs. 5). This means we are not to take away from another something that belongs to them.

It would be wrong if someone were to take my car and keep it from me. They would deprive me of what is mine, of what belongs to me. Likewise, a husband and wife should not deprive the other of what belongs to them, namely your body.

God intends for marriage to be permanent, and He intends for the sexual relationship within that marriage to be permanent. When you withhold yourself from your spouse, you rob them of that which Paul says is rightly theirs.

4. The consent of the married couple

Paul goes on to instruct married couples,

"Do not deprive one another except with consent for a time, that you may give yourselves to fasting and prayer; and come together again so that Satan does not tempt you because of your lack of self-control" (vs. 5).

As in all areas of life, our spiritual needs outrank our physical needs. Paul says that a married couple may abstain from the physical relationship only for the purpose of prayer and fasting, and only for a specific time period, and only if there is agreement in advance. The word *"consent"* used here means "sounding together." There is mutual understanding and mutual agreement.

There may be times in our life when we need to concentrate on a spiritual need. Prayer and fasting is a legitimate spiritual exercise. There are times when certain conditions in life necessitate that we focus solely on the spiritual.

After making this concession, Paul quickly warns against an extended time of abstinence. When the agreed period of time has expired, the married couple should resume normal physical relations. We must not leave Satan any room to tempt us.

Acts of consecration can set a trap for us if we allow them to carry us beyond the limits of our strength. The holding back of God-given desires can be as damaging as giving in to unrestrained desires.

There is a reluctance by some to preach on sex for fear of offending or alienating people. I would never want to do that. However, the subject of sex has been avoided in our churches because we have been taught to feel ashamed and guilty whenever we experience sexual desire. But by our silence, the church today allows the culture to define sex instead of the Bible defining it. Something is wrong when church is the only place where people don't hear about sex. Since God created it, since God ordained marriage so that we could live a life of purity and fulfillment, and since it is spoken of in the Bible, we should rejoice in the great gift that God has given to us. For more on the subject, I recommend the Song of Solomon.

The gifts God gives to us are good and perfect gifts. God has given to us the GIFT OF SEX that we might satisfy our flesh. However, God's greatest gift to us is the GIFT OF SALVATION through Jesus Christ our Lord to satisfy our soul. Won't you receive this gift today?

Good Housekeeping

Our modern society, with its political correctness and feminist organizations, would oppose any teaching that would encourage the submission of a wife to her husband. Even in the church many would oppose the submission of a wife to her husband. The church has been silent on the issue, perhaps for fear of offending people, or perhaps because they believe God's Word is no longer relevant to this contemporary society in which we live. Preaching on a wife's submissiveness is a sure way to increase a pastor's mail and e-mail.

A mail carrier said to the pastor of the church as he dropped off bags of mail, "Did you preach on wives being submissive to their husbands again?"

The apostle Paul, in writing to the church at Ephesus, gives to us inspired principles for good housekeeping. We will consider Paul's inspired principles for husbands in the next chapter, but for now let us consider Paul's instructions to wives regarding good housekeeping.

> Wives, submit to your own husbands, as to the Lord. For the husband is head of the wife, as also Christ is head of the church; and He is the Savior of the body. Therefore, just as the church is subject to Christ, so let the wives be to their own husbands in everything (Eph. 5:22-24).

Many women subscribe monthly to a magazine called *Good Housekeeping*. This magazine gives them recipes, ideas of how to decorate their home, etc. There was an article in *Housekeeping Monthly* in May of 1955, titled "The Good Wife's Guide." This article had eighteen recommendations for wives. Let me mention a few of these recommendations:

- Have dinner ready. Plan ahead, even the night before, to have a delicious meal ready, on time for his return.

- Take 15 minutes to rest so you'll be refreshed when he arrives. Touch up your makeup, put a ribbon in your hair and be fresh-looking.

- Be a little gay and a little more interesting for him. His boring day may need a lift and one of your duties is to provide it.

- Over the cooler months of the year you should prepare and light a fire for him to unwind by . . . catering for his comfort will provide you with immense personal satisfaction.

- Greet him with a warm smile and show sincerity in your desire to please him.

- Listen to him. Let him talk first - remember, his topics of conversation are more important than yours.

- Make the evening his. Never complain if he comes home late or goes out to dinner or other places of entertainment without you.

- Arrange his pillow and offer to take off his shoes. Speak in a low, soothing and pleasant voice.

- Don't ask him questions about his actions or question his judgment or integrity. Remember, he is the master of the house and as such will always exercise his will with fairness and truthfulness. You have no right to question him.

- A good wife always knows her place.

I wonder if a magazine would print that kind of advice to wives today? Well, of course not! Not that I agree with all of this, but this kind of talk would never do in a day of political correctness and feminism. Over the years magazines may change their tone on things, but the Bible has never changed its mind about anything! The Bible has said the same thing throughout the centuries. The contemporary is only temporary, but God and His Word are eternal.

The contemporary is only temporary,
but God and His Word are eternal.

Let us look at three things the apostle Paul says about good house-keeping:

1. The submission of the marriage

Paul says, *"Wives, submit to your own husbands, as to the Lord"* (vs. 22). Paul here is addressing wives. He is not addressing some wives, or a wife, but all believing wives. So if you're a wife, soon to be a wife, or ever want to be a wife, Paul's instruction is for you.

Let us note three things here about the submission of a wife.

A. The head of the wife

Paul says to all believing wives, *"submit to your own husbands."* The Greek word here for *"submit"* is "hupotasso," and it means "to subordinate; to obey; to be under obedience; submit self unto." It means to relinquish one's own rights, to willingly submit oneself.

A couple was celebrating their fiftieth wedding anniversary. Their domestic tranquility had long been the talk of the town. A local newspaper reporter was inquiring as to the secret of their long and happy marriage so he might write an article in the newspaper. "Well," said the wife, "it dates back to our honeymoon. We visited the Grand Canyon and took a trip down to the bottom of the canyon by pack mule. We hadn't gone too far when my husband's mule stumbled. My husband quietly said, 'That's once.' We proceeded a little farther when the mule stumbled again. Once more my husband quietly said, 'That's twice.' We hadn't gone a half-mile when the mule stumbled a third time. My husband took a pistol from his pocket and shot the mule. I began to protest over his cruel treatment of the mule when he looked at me and quietly said, 'That's once.'"

Husbands, that's not how God wants you to relate to your wife.

The question we must ask is this: Are submissiveness and inferiority synonymous? Our modern culture equates submissiveness with being inferior, and this is what disturbs people. Being submissive

Are submissiveness and inferiority synonymous?

does not make one inferior, and women are equal with men. This is clearly taught in the Bible. Paul said, *"There is neither Jew nor Greek, there is neither slave nor free, there is neither male nor female; for you are all one in Christ Jesus"* (Gal. 3:28).

Equality is not the issue. With everything God has created--the home, the church, the government--He has established order, organization, and leadership.

In the workplace all people are of equal value to God. The employee is not inferior to the boss. Both persons are of equal value. However, the employee is submissive to the direction of the boss.

Citizens are to be submissive to policemen. The law officer has been commissioned to exercise authority over us in order to preserve a peaceful society in which to live. Even though we are people of equal worth, we submit to the authority of the police officer, and we are adversely affected by those who do not.

Society requires that we live in submission with one another. If we neglect this universal principle, then we choose to live in a constant state of chaos and fear.

Submission is both biblical and practical. God established and ordained two institutions on earth: the family and the church. God gave both clear instructions on how He wants them to operate.

In the church we are all of equal value to the Lord. Jesus died for everyone of us and desires to save all mankind. But in the church, He has given oversight to those He has called out as pastors of the church. The scripture says, *"Obey those who rule over you and be submissive"* (Heb. 13:17).

In the home, all family members are of equal worth and value, but the Bible says that wives are to be submissive to the husband, and children are to be submissive to their parents.

In the Trinity, God the Father, God the Son, and God the Holy Ghost have coexisted and are coequal, yet Jesus the Son submitted to the will of God the Father and died on the cross.

The Scripture says here, "Wives, submit to your own husbands." This suggests intimacy. Husband and wife belong to each other in absolute equality. But for order and organization in the home, God has given the leadership to the husband.

B. The holiness of the wife

Let us notice Paul's words carefully, *"Wives, submit to your own husbands, as to the Lord"* (vs. 22). Paul not only gives wives a command here, he gives the motivation for obeying the command. A wife's submission to her husband is to be *"as to the Lord."* Paul says to the wives that their submission should not be for their husbands, or because of his worthiness, but for the Lord. What wife who loves Jesus does not want to please the Lord?

It is interesting that nowhere in the Gospels do we see a woman who opposes or ill-treats Jesus. Women honored Jesus; it was the men who opposed Jesus.

Peter said,

"For in this manner, in former times, the holy women who trusted in God also adorned themselves, being submissive to their own husbands as Sarah obeyed Abraham, calling him lord, whose daughters you are if you do good and are not afraid with any terror (1 Peter 3:5-6).

Just as Abraham is the father of faith, Sarah is the mother of submissiveness. *"Sarah obeyed Abraham."* She even called him *"lord."* This kind of attitude would be repulsive to today's feminist.

C. The home of the wife

In writing to Titus, Paul says,

"The older women likewise, that they be reverent in behavior . . . that they admonish the young women to love their husbands, to love their children, to be discreet, chaste, homemakers, good, obedient to their own husbands, that the word of God may not be blasphemed (Titus 2:3-5).

Wives are *"to love their husbands."* This love should not be based on his merit, but on God's command to do so. If you are a wife and you don't love your husband, you must train yourself to love him. This will involve praying for him and doing things for him even when you don't feel like it.

Wives are *"to love their children."* You are to love your children even when they are not lovable. Motherhood demands a selfless, sacrificial attitude. A wife should be careful not to put her children ahead of her husband.

I have a twin brother named Allan. One night as his wife, Linda, served the family dinner, their youngest child, Jacob, asked his mother, "Mom, why do you always serve dad first and give him the biggest piece of meat?" Before Linda could answer, Allan spoke up and said, "I can tell you why. You're just passing through, but I'm here to stay." Married couples would be wise to remember that they were together before any children came along, and they will be together after the children leave. The biblical principle of cleaving is for husbands and wives, not parents and children.

Wives are to be *"homemakers."* They are to be busy at home. Now I'm not saying that a wife and mother is to never work outside the home, but I am saying that the husband, the children, and the home are without question the number one priority of a woman because God has assigned no other work to the woman.

2. The structure of the marriage

After speaking to the submission of the marriage, Paul goes on to speak of the structure of the marriage. *"For the husband is head of the wife, as also Christ is head of the church; and He is the Savior of the body"* (vs. 23).

It's been said that marriage is the only union that can't be organized because both sides think they're in management.

We have been considering Paul's instructions to the church at Ephesus, but let's look at what he said to the church at Corinth:

"But I want you to know that the head of every man is Christ, the head of woman is man, and the head of Christ is God" (1 Cor. 11:3).

God is a God of order and He insists on order. Science tells us that there is order in the universe. The Bible tells us that there is order in the spirit world. In heaven there is the Trinity: God the Father, who is referred to as the first Person of the Trinity; Jesus the Son, who is referred to as the second Person of the Trinity; and the Holy Spirit, who is referred to as the third Person of the Trinity. Then there are angels, archangels, cherubim, and seraphim. The spirit world of darkness tries to imitate God's structure with Satan, the Antichrist, the false prophet, the fallen angels, and demons.

God's order for the family goes back to the garden of Eden. God created man first and woman second. Adam was given the place of head of the family. God said to Eve, *"Your desire shall be for your husband, and he shall rule over you"* (Gen. 3:16). The Hebrew word for "rule" used here literally means "dominion," inferring that Adam was to have power over Eve.

Ever since the fall of man there has been a power struggle between husbands and wives. The humorous story has been told that when everyone finally reached heaven, God instructed all the women to go with Saint Peter and for all the men to form two lines. One line was for those men who were dominated by their wives, and another line was for those men who ruled their wives. There was much movement, but eventually all the women are gone and all the men are in the two lines. The line of men who were dominated by their wives was hundreds of miles long. The line for men who ruled their wives had only one man in it. God told the men that they should be ashamed of themselves because He created them to rule their wives. Then He looked at the one man and said, "Learn from him!" He turned to the man and said, "Tell them, My son, how did you manage to be the only one in this line?" The man replied, "I don't know; my wife told me to stand here."

In creation, God established order. But, after the Fall, after sin entered the picture God told Eve that her desire would be toward her husband, meaning that she now would desire his power and position. Knowing this should help us better understand why many in the world promote a feminist agenda.

An ad appeared in a local newspaper that read:

FOR SALE BY OWNER
Complete set of Encyclopedia Britannica
45 volumes. Excellent condition. $1,000 or best offer.
No longer needed.
Got married last weekend. Wife knows everything.

Paul, in speaking to the churches at Ephesus and Corinth, is addressing those who are new creatures in Jesus Christ. Paul is stating that God is re-establishing the original order. Man is to be the head, under the Lordship of Jesus Christ. The wife is to recognize man's headship, which sounds chauvinistic to the unbeliever. Paul states very plainly the order: *"The head of every man is Christ, the head of woman is man, and the head of Christ is God"* (1 Cor. 11:3). We can ignore and disagree with God's order, but to do so will be to our own detriment. The Christian home is to be structured by the dictates of scripture, not by the dictates of society.

> *The Christian home is to be structured by the dictates of scripture, not by the dictates of society.*

When you buy an automobile, or an appliance, or a piece of machinery, it comes with an owner's manual. The manufacturer knows the operation of the equipment better than anyone, because the manufacturer made it or created it. It would be foolish to ignore the manufacturer's instructions.

When it comes to relationships, marriage, and the home, God is the manufacturer and He knows best. It would be foolish to ignore His instructions regarding the operation of our homes.

3. The sacredness of the marriage

The relationship between a husband and wife is a sacred relationship. Paul elevates the marital relationship to a high and lofty plane, *"Just as the church is subject to Christ, so let the wives be to their own husbands in everything"* (vs. 24). Just as the relationship between Christ and the church is sacred and special, the relationship between a husband and wife is to be sacred and special.

This sacred relationship is illustrated many times in scripture. Let me mention three relationships that picture the church's past, the church's present, and the church's future.

The church's past is seen in the relationship between Adam and Eve. The creation of Eve took place as *"God caused a deep sleep to fall on Adam"* (Gen. 2:21). God took from the side of Adam that which was needed to make him a bride and formed Eve.

The creation of the church took place as God *"gave His only begotten Son"* (Jn. 3:16). On the cross Jesus entered into the sleep of death, which was the will of God. The crucifixion account informs us that Jesus' side was opened. *"But one of the soldiers pierced His side with a spear, and immediately blood and water came out"* (Jn. 19:34). Out of Adam's side God took a rib and made him a bride. Out of Jesus' side God took blood, because *"without shedding of blood there is no remission"* (Heb. 9:22), and with this blood God made Jesus a bride . . . the church.

The church's present is seen in the relationship between Isaac and Rebekah. In Genesis 22, Isaac willingly laid on the altar and gave himself as a sacrifice. We turn a few pages, and in Genesis 24, Isaac has done all he can do. He now waits and watches as his father's unnamed servant goes to seek and to find a bride for him.

In this present age in which we live, Jesus has done all He can do. He willingly gave of Himself as a sacrifice for us. On the cross Jesus said, *"It is finished!"* (Jn. 19:30). On the day of Jesus' crucifixion, He could do no less than to bleed and die for our salvation, but today He can do no more for our salvation because *"It is finished!"* The work of salvation has been completed. Today Jesus sits at the right hand of God the Father waiting and watching as the Holy Spirit combs over the earth seeking the lost, inviting those to be the bride of Christ by accepting by faith His finished work on the cross.

The church's future is seen in the relationship between Joseph and Asenath. While in Egypt Joseph took a bride. Asenath was snatched out of obscurity and elevated to the lofty position as the bride of Joseph, Egypt's governor. What her life was like before being taken by Joseph, we don't know. The Scripture gives very little information about her. This we do know: From the moment Joseph took her, she would spend the rest of her days in the presence and fellowship of Joseph.

Egypt represents the world, and one day Jesus is going to come and take us out of this world. He is going to snatch us out of obscurity and elevate us to the lofty place of heaven. Whatever our life was like before won't matter any more. It won't matter if we were little known. All that will matter is that we will spend eternity in the presence and fellowship of Him who is King of kings and Lord of lords! Hallelujah, what a Savior!

Good housekeeping means that we do things God's way. There is to be submission in the home, there is to be structure in the home, and there is to be sacredness in the home.

When a Man
Loves a Woman

In Ephesians 5, Paul addresses husbands. If you are a husband, or some day plan to be a husband, then listen up. Paul does not offer suggestions here; he is commanding husbands to love their wives.

> Husbands, love your wives, just as Christ also loved the church and gave Himself for her, that He might sanctify and cleanse her with the washing of water by the word, that He might present her to Himself a glorious church, not having spot or wrinkle or any such thing, but that she should be holy and without blemish. So husbands ought to love their own wives as their own bodies; he who loves his wife loves himself. For no one ever hated his own flesh, but nourishes and cherishes it, just as the Lord does the church. For we are members of His body, of His flesh and of His bones. "For this reason a man shall leave his father and mother and be joined to his wife, and the two shall become one flesh." This is a great mystery, but I speak concerning Christ and the church. Nevertheless let each one of you in particular so love his own wife as himself, and let the wife see that she respects her husband (Eph. 5:25-33).

The last statistic I read indicates that about forty percent of marriages in America end in divorce. Many would claim that the institution of marriage has crashed to the ground, killing multitudes of people. Therefore, many have abandoned marriage believing it is no longer relevant, while others have fought and pushed for alternatives to the traditional one-man and one-woman marriage. Today in the United States we are only a couple of legislative votes away from having homosexual marriage imposed as the law of the land in all fifty states, without one state ever having approved this radical idea at the ballot box.

But upon closer review we will discover that it is not the institution of marriage that has failed but the individuals in those marriages that have failed. We do not need to abandon the institution of marriage, but we do need to take drastic steps to fix the problem.

One thing we can do is to let our representatives know how we feel about protecting the institution of marriage and that we expect them to represent us in any, and all, marriage protection legislation.

When I fly, I mostly fly Delta Airlines. If forty percent of Delta's flights crashed to the ground, drastic measures would be taken to correct the problem. Upon close review, what if the authorities discovered that it was not the planes which malfunctioned. It was the pilots who did not follow proper procedures and thereby lost control of the plane, killing multitudes of people.

You see it is not the institution of marriage that has failed. It is the individuals in marriages who ignore the instructions of God who created marriage. For marriage to be successful, we must heed the instruction of Him who created marriage!

How can you know when a man loves a woman?

Let us look at three indicators which reveal a husband's love for his wife:

1. The husband's initiation

In this Ephesian passage we find the word *"love"* mentioned six times. Husbands, please note that the word *"love"* used here by Paul is not an eros love, an erotic love. It is not a phileo love, a friendly love or a fond love. The word used here by Paul is an agape love, the highest kind of love. A godly and sacrificial love. It carries the idea of making much of a person.

After marriage, some men show more attention and affection to their cars, boats, golf clubs, and hobbies than they do to their wives.

One man had a love affair with his car, and he wanted to make their relationship official. After his girlfriend had dumped him, he tried to marry his true love, which was his 1996 Mustang. He went to the courthouse and tried to marry his car. He filled out a marriage application before the clerk put an end to his dream. On this application he listed his fiance's birthdate as "1996," her birthplace as "Detroit," her father as "Henry Ford" and her blood type as "10-W-40."

Let us note two things about the husband's initiative:

A. The apostle's degree

The apostle Paul says to husbands, *"Husbands, love your wives"* (vs. 25). This is no suggestion or recommendation; it is a command!

The Bible commands us to love the Lord. When asked what was the greatest commandment, Jesus said,

"You shall love the LORD your God with all your heart, with all your soul, and with all your mind" (Matt. 22:37).

Just as we have been commanded to love the Lord, husbands have been commanded to love their wives. Paul didn't say we are to love her only if she is lovely. Paul didn't say we are to love her when she is submissive. Paul said we are to love her--period! A husband is without excuse when it comes to loving his wife.

Husbands are to initiate love. Just as Christ initiated His love to us, husbands are to take the initiative in loving their wives.

B. The husband's demonstration

Paul goes on to say, *"Husbands, love your wives, just as Christ also loved the church and gave Himself for her."* Jesus initiated a relationship with us while we were still sinners. Jesus is sinless, we are sinful, yet He gave Himself for us. He took the initiative. *But God demonstrates His own love toward us, in that while we were still sinners, Christ died for us* (Rom. 5:8).

How can we be sure of God's love for us? We can know that God loves us, because while in our sin He demonstrated His love for us by giving to us His Son and His salvation.

Husband, one of the greatest ways that you demonstrate your love for your wife is to initiate the restoration of your relationship when differences surface. To do so will often mean that you will have to swallow your pride. But remember, before honor comes humiliation. Today we honor Jesus, but before this honor came His humiliation on the cross.

Husband, when you and your wife have an argument, you should initiate reconciliation with her. "But," you say, "it was her fault." I have been married for thirty-two years. Every disagreement or debate that my wife and I have had, it has been her fault. At least from my perspective! Obviously, if I didn't think she was wrong, I wouldn't be at odds with her. However, a husband's role is to be like Jesus. He took the initiative to restore the relationship with us when we were at fault. Jesus is sinless, and we are sinful. Yet we have a relationship with Him today because of His initiation.

A husband's role is to be like Jesus.

This is a tough principle for men. Male pride makes this a hard pill to swallow. This is contrary to the flesh. Husbands, you will never be successful with this principle apart from the filling of the Holy Spirit. The fruit of the Spirit is love, long-suffering, gentleness or meekness (Gal. 5:22-23). Apart from the Holy Spirit a husband has no chance to relate to his bride as Christ has related to His bride, the church.

Paul said just as Christ *"gave Himself"* for the church, husbands are to give themselves to their wives.

In Judges 14 we find an interesting story of Samson. Samson wanted to take a gentile wife and was willing to give himself to get her. In this way, Samson is a type of Christ. On his way to getting a gentile wife, Samson was met by a lion who came against him. Samson killed the lion with his bare hands and went on his way to get this gentile bride who was undeserving of him. When Samson met her she could see from the marks on his body that he was willing to give himself to have her. In this way, Samson demonstrated his love for her.

Jesus has demonstrated His love for us. On Jesus' way to getting Himself a bride, He was met by the cross. His body bears the marks of the cross demonstrating His love for His bride, the church.

A husband is to love his wife in such a way that he would give himself for her. Once again, male pride must be defeated. When Paul said that Jesus *"gave Himself for her,"* he was saying that Jesus surrendered Himself for His bride. The word *"gave"* here means surrender.

Just as we must surrender ourselves and make ourselves less of a priority so that we can live for Christ, a husband is to surrender himself for his wife.

In St. Petersburg, Russia, zoo officials implemented a plan to introduce orangutans to the joys of family life by having them watch television together. The scheme backfired, however, because the male orangutan soon got so engrossed in TV that his mate became jealous and upset. The zoo director announced they would reduce the hours of television watched in an attempt to salvage the relationship.[1]

Husbands, why don't you take the initiative and cut some things out of your lives that are upsetting to your wives, and enhance your marital relationship.

2. The husband's imitation

In Ephesians 5 Paul holds Jesus Christ up as the husband's example. The husband is to look at Jesus' relationship with His bride, the church, and imitate that in his relationship with his bride.

Paul has been speaking about a husband's bride; now he speaks of a husband's body. In both instances, Paul uses Jesus as the husband's example.

Let us note some ways in which a husband is to imitate Christ.

A. A husband is to care for his wife.

A husband is to take care of his wife in the same way he would take care of his own body. You see, when you get married, you become one flesh. Paul instructed the Corinthians that upon marriage the wife's body no longer belonged to her but to her husband, and the husband's body no longer belonged to him but to his wife (1 Cor. 7:4). Therefore, a husband is to care for his wife as he would care for himself.

Could you imagine your eye hating your mouth? The eye would see something poisonous, yet communicate to the body that it would be delicious to eat. So the mouth would eat it only to discover that it had an awful taste and is fatal to the body. The eye's dislike for the mouth ended up causing trouble for the eye as well as the rest of the body.

We should love the church as ourselves because as believers we are a part of the body of Christ. We are to love the church of Jesus Christ. We are to love fellow believers because we are a part of same body. In like manner, a husband is to love his wife, for she is a part of him. For a husband to come against his wife is the same as coming against himself because they are the same flesh.

Just as Jesus could not harm His bride (the church), a husband could not harm his bride. When she needs encouragement, he is to give her encouragement. When she needs strength, he is to give her strength.

Paul wrote to the Philippians,

And my God shall supply all your need according to His riches in glory by Christ Jesus (Phil. 4:19).

Just as Jesus, the Bridegroom, supplies our needs as His bride, husbands are to supply the needs of their wives. Something is wrong when a husband looks at his wife only as a cook, housekeeper, and sex partner. She is to be his most prized possession, and he is to care for her.

B. A husband is to cherish his wife.

A husband is to cherish his wife. In attitude he is to hold her dear. In action he is to treat her with affection. Paul said,

"For no one ever hated his own flesh, but nourishes and cherishes it, just as the Lord does the church" (vs. 29).

A woman was arrested for shoplifting. When she went before the judge he asked her, "What did you steal?" She replied, "A can of peaches." The judge asked her why she had stolen them, and she said she was hungry. The judge then asked her how many peaches were in the can. She replied, "Six." The judge then said, "I will give you six days in jail."

Before the judge could actually pronounce the sentence, the woman's husband spoke up and asked the judge if he could say something. The judge said to him, "What is it?" The husband said, "Judge, she also stole a can of peas."

A husband is to cherish his wife, nourish his wife, and provide for his wife.

A 92-year old man named Luther was engaged to an 89-year old woman named Louella. Now Luther was all excited about their wedding but also concerned because he knew he was to take care of Louella and provide for her. So Luther visited his pharmacist and asked him several questions. Luther said, "I am about to get married to an 89-year old woman and need to know if you sell heart medication." The pharmacist said, "Of course we do."

Luther asked, "How about medicine for circulation?" The pharmacist replied, "All kinds."

Luther then asked, "How about medicine for rheumatism, arthritis, and scoliosis?" The pharmacist answered, "Definitely."

Luther asked, "How about medicine for memory problems and jaundice?" The pharmacist replied, "Yes, a large variety. The works."

Luther continued, "How about vitamins, sleeping pills, and Geritol?" The pharmacist replied, "Absolutely."

Luther then asked, "How about wheelchairs and walkers?" The pharmacist replied, "All speeds and sizes."

Finally, Luther said to the pharmacist, "I would like to use your pharmacy as our Bridal registry."

Just as the church is dear to Jesus, a wife is to be dear to her husband. The husband is to love and cherish his wife, imitating Christ's love for the church.

A husband's love for his wife should be . . .

1) Sacrificial

Jesus gave Himself for the church. A husband should give himself to his wife.

Jesus sacrificed Himself and gave His blood and His life for His bride. Adam sacrificed himself and gave a rib for his bride. Jacob sacrificed fourteen years to have Rachel for his wife. It's no wonder he loved her more than Leah, whom he got at no cost.

A husband cannot love his wife sacrificially unless he is submitted to Christ and filled with the Holy Spirit. You cannot love like Christ if you are not submitted to Him.

2) Sanctifying

Jesus loved the church so that *"He might sanctify and cleanse her"* (vs. 26). To sanctify means to set apart. Jesus loves us and sets us apart from, and above, the world. Be careful not to belittle the Lord's church, because Jesus makes much of His bride.

A husband is to so love his wife that his love for her sets her apart from, and above, all others. A husband's love is to make much of his wife.

3) Satisfying

A husband should so love his wife that she is satisfied. Paul says that a husband *"nourishes"* his wife. Nourishment is necessary for life and growth. The opposite of nourishment is starvation.

There are a lot of marriages where the wife is not nourished, where she is not satisfied. In fact, she is starving and craving for her husband's love.

A husband should satisfy his wife emotionally, physically, and spiritually.

3. The husband's inspiration

How do you know when a man loves a woman? When he is the initiator in maintaining a healthy marital relationship. You know that a husband loves his wife when he imitates Jesus' love for the church as the model for his love for his wife. And you know that a husband loves his wife because his love for her inspires her to revere him. The reason many wives do not respect their husbands is because the husband is not loving her as he should.

Paul says that when a husband loves his wife as he loves himself, the wife will respect her husband. The King James Version puts it this way, *"and the wife see that she reverence her husband"* (vs. 33), which means "to be in awe."

You see, the reason I am in awe regarding Jesus Christ is because He has loved me in such a godly, undeserving way that His love has overwhelmed me.

Husbands, when you love your wives as Paul has commanded, she will put you up on a pedestal and admire you. When you initiate and maintain a healthy relationship with your wife, when you imitate the love of Jesus in your home, you will inspire your wife and she will respect you.

In most marriages it may be difficult for a wife to revere her husband, but for a wife not to revere her husband is disastrous.

Husbands, think about your wife as you read this:

I May Not Have Another Chance

If I knew it would be the last time that I'd see you fall asleep,

I would tuck you in more tightly and pray the Lord, your soul to keep.

If I knew it would be the last time that I would see you walk out the door,

I would give you a hug and kiss and call you back for one more.

If I knew it would be the last time I'd hear your voice lifted up in praise,

I would video tape each action and word, so I could play them back day after day.

If I knew it would be the last time that I would have the opportunity to tell you,

I would say, "I love you," and would not assume that you knew.

If I knew it would be the last time that together we would spend the day,

I would make the most of every minute and not let even one slip away.

But surely there is always tomorrow to make up for an oversight.

Surely I will get a second chance to make things right.

But just in case I might be wrong, and today is all I get,

I'd like to say how much I love you and hope we never forget,

Tomorrow is not promised to anyone, young and old alike,

And today may be the last chance I get to hold you tight.

So if you're waiting for tomorrow, why not do it today? For if tomorrow never comes, you'll surely regret the day,

That you didn't take that extra time for a smile, a hug, or a kiss,

And you were too busy to grant your wife, what turned out to be her one last wish.

So hold your wife close today and whisper in her ear,

Tell her how much you love her and that you'll always hold her dear,

Take time to say "I'm sorry," "please forgive me," "thank you," or "it's okay."

And if tomorrow never comes, you'll have no regrets about today.

1. World, Jan. 16, 1999 (page 13)

Planned Parenthood

Today we have the ungodly organization in our society called Planned Parenthood. An organization that encourages alternatives to childbirth such as abortion and contraceptives. My one and only visit to their web site was interesting. Their web site promotes abortion, the morning-after pill, contraceptives and, of course, their propaganda. One of their links is "George W. Bush's War on Women." This link takes you to the article, "The War on Women: A Chronology." The article begins, "In recent years the Executive and Legislative branches of our federal government have been waging a war on women and their reproductive rights.

"Retrograde anti-choice policies are being revived. Religious political extremists have been given key administration positions." They cite various appointments, policies, and budgeting issues that the administration has made with which they disagree. They are too numerous for me to mention them all, but here is one example:

"House passes the 'Child Custody Protection Act,' which would make it a federal crime to transport a minor across state lines for an abortion unless the parental involvement requirements of her home state have been met (April 17, 2002)."

Now when it comes to parenting, you can look to Planned Parenthood, or you can look to God and His Word! There have been many books, seminars, and web sites on the family and how to raise kids. Yet nothing compares to the Word of God as our basis for any and all relationships, especially in the home.

God has ordained the home and the church, and He tells us how to relate to each other in both places.

Parenthood becomes a reality when you experience one or more of the following:

- You eat dinner on Dora the Explorer or Bob the Builder plates.

- You choose a restaurant because it has a playground.

- You catch yourself singing the "Barney" theme song . . . in public.

- You find yourself watching cartoons even when your kids aren't in the room.

- You buy breakfast cereal according to the characters on the box.

- You stay in your pajamas most days because getting everyone ready is just not worth the fight.

- You have the total collection of McDonald's plates and drinking glasses.

- Your idea of a nice dinner out is to go to Chuck E Cheese.

- Your living room has been turned into an indoor basketball court or a make-believe beauty shop.

- The only band-aid in the house has Spiderman on it.

- You take phone messages with a crayon.

- You pack six suitcases to go on a three-day trip.

- You do the potty celebration dance with your child in public after a successful trip to the restroom.

- You find yourself cutting your spouse's meal into bite-sized pieces.

- Your cologne or perfume smells like spit-up,

In Paul's letter to the church at Ephesus we find God's plan for parenthood.

Children, obey your parents in the Lord, for this is right. "Honor your father and mother," which is the first commandment with promise: "that it may be well with you and you may live long on the earth." And you, fathers, do not provoke your children to wrath, but bring them up in the training and admonition of the Lord (Eph. 6:1-4).

Let us consider four things about God's plan for parenthood.

1. The conformity of children

The apostle Paul has previously given a command to the wives,

"Wives, submit to your own husbands, as to the Lord" (5:22).

Paul also commanded the husbands,

"Husbands, love your wives, just as Christ also loved the church and gave Himself for her" (5:25).

Now Paul commands children,

"Children, obey your parents in the Lord, for this is right" (6:1).

Paul didn't command parents, "Parents, obey your children and make them happy in every way." No! Paul said, *"Children, obey your parents."* The word *"obey"* means "to hear under (as a subordinate), to listen attentively, to heed or conform to a command."

A child is to obey his parents' authority. It is very important that children submit to, and obey, the authority of their parents. Later on in life they will have authorities in school, in government, and in employment. How will a child grow up to respect these authorities when he does not respect the authority of his parents?

As a child grows and matures, parents stand in the gap and intercede for them until they can develop their own relationship with the Lord. Children who defy and disobey their parents will go on to defy and disobey other authorities, and will most likely go on to defy and disobey God.

A young boy had just gotten his driving permit. He asked his father if they could discuss the use of the car. His father said to him, "I'll make a deal with you. You bring your grades up, study your Bible more, and get a hair cut, then we'll talk about it."

A month later the boy came back and again asked his father if they could discuss the use of the car. The father said to his son, "Son, I've been real proud of you. You have brought your grades up, you've been studying your Bible, but you have not gotten a hair cut!"

> *Children who defy and disobey their parents will go on to defy and disobey other authorities.*

The son said to his dad, "You know, Dad, I've been thinking about that. Samson had long hair, Moses had long hair, Noah had long hair, and even Jesus had long hair." The father then said, "Yes, I know, and they walked everywhere they went!"

Paul instructs children what they are to do: obey their parents. He also instructs them why they are to do it: for the Lord's sake. A wife is to submit to her husband *"as to the Lord"* (5:22). A husband is to love his wife *"as Christ also loved the church"* (5:25). Now Paul instructs children to obey their parents *"in the Lord"* (6:1).

A child's obedience to his or her parents is a demonstration of their obedience to the Lord. Wives are to submit to their husbands because God asks it of them, not because the husband deserves it. Husbands are to love their wives because God asks it of them, not because the wife deserves it. Children are to obey their parents because God asks it of them, not because the parents deserve it. For a wife not to submit to her husband, for a husband not to love his wife, and for a child not to obey his parents is to disobey God!

How can a child conform to God's authority when he will not conform to his parents' authority?

Jesus is the child's example. We have only one glimpse of Jesus' childhood. As a twelve year old, Jesus knew He was the Son of God. At twelve He was teaching in the temple and doing *"His Father's business"* (Lk. 2:49). Yet the Scripture is careful to tell us that Jesus was *"subject"* or obedient, to Mary and Joseph, His earthly parents (Lk. 2:51). Just think about it. Here is the One who is from everlasting to everlasting. He is the Creator, the Lord of glory, the King of kings, and the Lord of lords! Yet He subjects Himself to, and obeys, a village carpenter and his peasant wife.

2. The command to children

While speaking to children, Paul quotes the fifth of the Ten Commandments.

> "Honor your father and mother," which is the first commandment with promise" (Eph. 6:2).

Every one of the Ten Commandments is repeated in the New Testament except for the fourth commandment, which says to *"Remember the Sabbath day"* (Ex. 20:8). Disobedience for the New Testament Christian is just as wrong as it was for the Old Testament Jew.

The division of the Ten Commandments has often been a topic of interest. Some would divide the commandments into two parts. The first part, which consists of the first four commandments, emphasizes man's relationship with God. The second part, which consists of the last six commandments, emphasizes man's relationship with man. I believe the Ten Commandments are divided in the middle. I believe the first five commandments emphasize man's relationship with God, because in each one we find the words, *"the Lord your God"* (Ex. 20:2,

5, 7, 8, 12). The last five commandments emphasize man's relationship with man, because in each one we find the words, *"You shall not"* (Ex. 20:13, 14, 15, 16, 17).

This is important because the fifth commandment which Paul quotes here in his instruction to children comes from the first half of the Ten Commandments, which emphasizes man's relationship with God.

A child's obedience has more to do with their relationship with God than it does with their relationship with their parents. Parents, you need to understand this principle. If you desire to raise godly children, you must be unwavering regarding their obedience to you.

A child's obedience has more to do with their relationship with God than it does with their relationship with their parents.

When my daughters were still at home they would come to me with some request. They would say, "Dad, could I do this, or could I do that?" I learned over time to respond by saying, "Well, talk to God. If it's all right with God it will be all right with me." One time one of them said, "Dad, you know that wouldn't be all right with God." I replied, "Then what are you asking me for?" As parents, we need to teach our children that ultimately, they will answer to God. We need to raise them to live for God and to stand before God. But until a child grows to be accountable to God, this fifth commandment puts parents in the place of God over their children.

When a child rebels or disobeys their parents, it is an insult to God who placed the parent over the child and gave that parent authority. When children disobey their parents, they sin against God Himself.

Paul says to children, *"Honor your father and mother."* The word *"honor"* used here means "To prize, fix a valuation, to revere." Children, you are to prize and revere your parents.

One way children can honor their parents is to see after them in their elderly years, caring and providing for them when they are no longer capable of doing so themselves. Just as parents spend time and money caring for their young children who cannot care for themselves, in like manner, children should spend whatever time and money is necessary to care for their parents when they reach the point that they can no longer care for themselves.

A parent should be careful not to ignore their responsibility by constantly pushing their young kids off on others. When a parent gets old those same kids might ignore their responsibility by pushing their older parents off on someone else. When you raise your children with the idea that it is the government's job, or the school's job, or the church's job to raise your kids, those same kids may later in life believe it is the responsibility of some convalescent home, or some other institution, to take care of you.

3. The crown of children

What is the crown, the reward, for children? *"That it may be well with you and you may live long on the earth"* (Eph. 6:3). This verse gives great promise for those children who obey and honor their parents. This verse promises quality of life, *"that it may be well with you."* The word *"well"* means "good, well done." This verse promises quantity of life, *"you may live long on the earth."*

A child who obeys this command and honors his or her mother and father provides the foundation for a life of satisfaction, stability, and success. The disobedient, disrespectful child can look forward to depression, disappointment, and dissatisfaction.

From the example of Jesus, we learn that children are to grow in four ways which we see from the life of Jesus.

And Jesus increased in wisdom and stature, and in favor with God and men (Luke 2:52).

Children are to grow intellectually.

A baby is born with a blank mind. Parents are to teach and stimulate the intellect of their children. One of the greatest robbers of intellectual development is the TV. We have substituted education with entertainment.

Children are to grow physically.

Obviously Jesus grew from a babe in Bethlehem's manger to a man who walked among us. Babies grow as they are fed, and it is the parents' responsibility to see to their child's diet.

Children are to grow socially.

Parents should raise their children to get along with others. A child is born with the unbecoming characteristic of selfishness. A child must be taught cooperation and consideration.

Children are to grow spiritually.

A child doesn't just naturally develop to know God. Just as a child must be physically fed to grow, they must be spiritually fed to grow. That is why preschool teachers in our church are required to teach and sing about Jesus.

Children should be well-bred, well-fed, well-read, well-led, well-wed, so that one day they will be well-dead.

"Jesus increased in wisdom and stature, and in favor with God and men." This word *"increased"* means "to drive forward, to advance, to grow, to be well along." I believe this is referring to Jesus' human nature.

Isn't it interesting that the Bible says that *"Jesus increased in . . .*

favor with God"? The verse before says that Jesus *"was subject"* (was obedient) to His earthly parents (Lk. 2:51-52). As a child, Jesus found favor with God because He was obedient to His earthly parents. No wonder Paul commanded, *"Children, obey your parents in the Lord, for this is right."*

4. The correction of children

Paul has given instructions to wives, to husbands, to children, and now to fathers or parents.

> And you, fathers, do not provoke your children to wrath, but bring them up in the training and admonition of the Lord (Eph. 6:4).

This verse instructs parents to do two things:

Parents are to direct their children.

We don't need reform in the educational system today; we need reform in the parental system today. We don't need better curriculum in our schools today; we need better character and better childhood in our homes today.

One hundred years from now it will not matter what kind of car you drove, or what kind of house you lived in, or how much money was in your bank account. But one hundred years from now the world could be better because as a parent you were important in the life of your child.

The word *"training"* or *"nurture"* (KJV) means "tutorage, education or training, disciplinary correction, chastening."

There is much emphasis in the Old Testament on a child's spiritual upbringing. One such example is found regarding Israel's annual Passover Feast. This feast would not only remind Israel of God's deliverance from slavery and bondage, it would also serve to teach the children who would not understand and would ask questions of their parents (Ex. 13:8).

By the way, this is why I do not prefer a "Children's Church." Children's Church shifts the responsibility from parent to church. When something happens in church that a child does not understand, it provides a great opportunity for the parent to teach, instruct, and explain to the child.

Parents are to discipline their children.

Have you ever run across a 250-pound man who says he cannot control his 60-pound kid? The kid is a brat and his father says he cannot do anything about it.

A parent who loves his child will discipline his child. God disciplines His children because He loves them. Love motivates us to discipline. The absence of love motivates us to ignore our children and to abuse them. Solomon said,

> "Foolishness is bound up in the heart of a child; The rod of correction will drive it far from him" (Prov. 22:15).

One woman approached a mother with her young son and said, "My, your child is well-behaved, and he's loaded with self-esteem! Do you applaud him often?" The mother replied, "Yes, with one hand!"

In his commentary on Ephesians, Warren Wiersbe quotes the Duke of Windsor from years ago who said, "Everything in the American home is controlled by switches - except the children!"

"Everything in the American home is controlled by switches – except the children!"

General Douglas MacArthur, a five-star general, a distinguished leader and patriot, and an American hero, was also a conscientious father. During his time in the Far East during World War II, General MacArthur wrote this prayer:

"Build me a son, O Lord, who will be strong enough to know when he is weak, and brave enough to face himself when he is afraid; one who will be proud and unbending in honest defeat, and humble and gentle in victory. Build me a son whose wishbone will not be where his backbone should be; a son who will know Thee and that to know himself is the foundation stone of knowledge. Lead him I pray, not in the path of ease and comfort, but under the stress and spur of difficulties and challenge. Here let him learn to stand up in the storm; here let him learn compassion for those who fail. Build me a son whose heart will be clear, whose goal will be high; a son who will master himself before he seeks to master other men; one who will learn to laugh, yet never forget how to weep; one who will reach into the future, yet never forget the past.

"And after all these things are his, add, I pray, enough of a sense of humor, so that he may always be serious, yet never take himself too seriously. Give him humility, so that he may always remember the simplicity of true greatness, the open mind of true wisdom, the meekness of true strength. Then, I, his father, will dare to whisper, I have not lived in vain."

God has a plan for parenthood, and we need to know and apply His plan. God also has a plan whereby He can be your heavenly Father and you can be His child. The apostle Paul wrote,

"The Spirit Himself bears witness with our spirit that we are children of God" (Rom. 8:16).

To be a child of your father, you must be born into his family. To be a child of God, the heavenly Father, Jesus said,

"You must be born again" (Jn. 3:7).

The Faith of Parents

When popular radio talk show therapist, Dr. Laura Schlessinger criticized day care on the Phil Donahue Show a few years ago, the audience became hostile. But she quickly turned the tables by challenging them, "If you were going to wake up tomorrow morning as an infant, would you choose to be raised by a day-care center, a nanny, or a baby-sitter rather than by your parents? If so, stand up now!" Nobody stood.

Children were given to parents, and parents are to care for their children.

Hebrews 11 is referred to as the faith chapter where we find the heroes of faith. Although not named, the only parents we find among the heroes of our faith listed in this great chapter are Moses' father and mother, Amram and Jochebed.

Moses' parents are not found in Hebrews 11 because they were great preachers or singers. Nor did they run a successful, multimillion dollar company, or ever aspire to a political office. Yet they are mentioned among the heroes of our faith because they were parents who had faith in God and passed that faith on to their son Moses. Their parenting made a difference in the world, both then and today.

According to Scripture parents have the primary responsibility for teaching their children (Deut. 6:4-9).

If your child had perfect attendance in Sunday School, they would get about 52 hours of Bible study a year. However, there are 8,760 hours in a year. Sunday School represents only 0.59%, or just over one half of one percent of time in a year. In a year's time, children spend much more time watching commercials on TV than they spend in

Sunday School. Time is precious. We must make the most of it by passing our faith along to our children.

Let's read about Moses and his parents from Hebrews 11.

By faith Moses, when he was born, was hidden three months by his parents, because they saw he was a beautiful child; and they were not afraid of the king's command. By faith Moses, when he became of age, refused to be called the son of Pharaoh's daughter, choosing rather to suffer affliction with the people of God than to enjoy the passing pleasures of sin, esteeming the reproach of Christ greater riches than the treasures in Egypt; for he looked to the reward. By faith he forsook Egypt, not fearing the wrath of the king; for he endured as seeing Him who is invisible. By faith he kept the Passover and the sprinkling of blood, lest he who destroyed the firstborn should touch them. By faith they passed through the Red Sea as by dry land, whereas the Egyptians, attempting to do so, were drowned (Hebrews 11:23-29).

The faith of parents is crucial in the life of children. We see four things that faced Moses, and will face every child, which demands that we be people of faith:

1. The dangers of this world

The explosion of the Hebrew population caused much concern for the Egyptian pharaoh. He made into law that all male babies must be drowned in the Nile River. But *"by faith Moses, when he was born, was hidden three months by his parents"* (vs. 23). The faith of Amram and Jochebed made them unafraid of the Pharaoh's command. They feared God more than they feared Pharaoh.

The psalmist said,

"Though an army may encamp against me, My heart shall not fear (Psa. 27:3). In God I have put my trust; I will not fear (Psa. 56:4). The fear of the LORD is the beginning of wisdom" (Psa. 111:10).

Parents, we are not to fear, or be frightened by man if we fear, or revere, the Lord. Without this reverence to God we will give in to the pressures of this world.

Amram and Jochebed were not afraid of Pharaoh and his commands because they revered the Lord. They knew, by faith, that God had created their child, Moses, and that God had great plans for him. Their attention was given to saving his life.

Because of Pharoah's edict, Moses, along with other Hebrew male babies, was born a condemned person. How does God save a person that is condemned? Perhaps Amram and Jochebed thought back to Noah and the ark. When all the people of the world died in the waters of death, Noah was saved by the ark. Now that Pharaoh had commanded the death of Hebrew boys in the waters of the Nile, Amram and Jochebed built for Moses an *"ark of bulrushes"* (Ex. 2:3). Just as God used Noah to save the human race, by faith Amram and Jochebed believed God would use Moses to save the Hebrew race.

It must be pointed out that when our children are born, much like Moses they are condemned--they are born with a sin nature. This is why Jesus said,

"For God did not send His Son into the world to condemn the world, but that the world through Him might be saved" (Jn. 3:17).

Jesus did not leave the glory of heaven in order that He might come to this world and condemn us. He didn't have to do that because we stood condemned already. Jesus came to save us from sin's condemnation. Noah was saved because he found safety and security in the ark. Baby Moses was saved because he found safety and security in the ark of bulrushes. We are saved when we find safety and security in Christ Jesus!

It is no wonder that Moses was a man of great faith. His parents had great faith. Moses' parents were willing to risk their own lives in order to follow God. Years later Moses would risk his life in order to follow God.

Moses' parents must have been reassured of their faith when a princess, Pharaoh's own daughter, found Moses and wanted to raise him as her own child. And then Miriam, Moses' sister, persuaded the princess to get Jochebed to nurse the baby Moses.

> *Parents, what are you believing God for regarding your child or children?*

Moses' parents believed that God had a purpose for their son, and their actions revealed their faith. Parents, what are you believing God for regarding your child or children? God has a purpose for your child's existence. God has a plan for each and every person. Amram and Jochebed's actions complemented their belief that God had a plan for their son.

Our parenting as Christians should be based on the fact that God has a plan for each child. Our parenting should not be based on our child being a cheerleader, or a star athlete, or a famous person, or a rich person. The motivation and basis for our parenting is the fact that God has a plan for the life of our child. To that end we must raise our children. Like Amram and Jochebed, a parent should have their eyes on a greater King than Pharaoh.

The life of Moses teaches us that children learn what they live:

Raise a child with criticism and he learns to condemn.

Raise a child with hostility and he learns to fight.

Raise a child with ridicule and he learns to be shy.

Raise a child with encouragement and he learns to be confident.

Raise a child with tolerance and he learns to be patient.

Raise a child with praise and he learns to appreciate.

Raise a child with honesty and he learns what truth is.

Raise a child with acceptance and he learns to love.

Raise a child with fairness and he learns justice.

Raise a child with friendliness and he learns that the world is a nice place in which to live.

Raise a child with faith and he learns how to walk with God.

2. The disguise of this world

Satan and the world will disguise themselves to become attractive. For Moses, the world offered him everything.

Every parent needs to notice what happened here. We first read about the faith of Moses' parents in verse 23. The very next verse, verse 24, tells us about Moses' faith. Moses had faith and faith moved him into action, *"by faith he forsook Egypt"* (vs. 27).

The crucial point in a relay race is when one runner passes the baton to another runner. That transition must go well for there to be hope of victory. In like manner, it is crucial that the parents pass the torch of faith to the next generation.

How can you ever know if you are a good parent? How can you know if you have successfully passed on the baton of faith? I think the best way to know is when we watch our children pass the baton of faith on to their children.

Amram and Jochebed's faith caused them to ignore the evil command of Pharaoh. Moses' faith caused him to forsake the offerings of the world and to turn his back on Egypt. We see here the passing of faith from one generation to the next.

Parents should teach their children to refuse . . .

1) *Worldly position.*

By faith Moses, when he became of age, refused to be called the son of Pharaoh's daughter (vs. 23).

As the adopted son of Pharaoh's daughter, Moses had every reason to believe that he could become the next pharaoh and sit on the throne of Egypt. Surely the devil must have tempted him by saying, "Once we can get you on the throne, you can be of much help for your people, the Jews. God needs men like you in high positions."

How often we compromise when Satan offers us something that is both of value and appeals to our flesh. Moses would not hear of it. He knew that was not God's way. Satan can never offer you something that is good, or right, or God's will. Jesus has already told us that:

"The thief does not come except to steal, and to kill, and to destroy" (Jn. 10:10).

Moses *"refused to be called the son of Pharaoh's daughter."* The word *"refused"* used here means "to contradict." The princess would introduce Moses as her son, and Moses would contradict her.

Parents should teach their children to refuse worldly position when that position conflicts with God's plan.

2) *Worldly pleasures.*

Moses chose *rather to suffer affliction with the people of God than to enjoy the passing pleasures of sin* (vs. 25). Moses was raised to have such faith that he would rather be right with God and suffer than to enjoy the fleeting pleasure of sin. Moses' parents had raised him to understand that sin is short-lived in pleasure, but long-lived in consequences.

3) *Worldly prosperity.*

Moses esteemed *the reproach of Christ's greater riches than the treasures in Egypt; for he looked to the reward* (vs. 26). Everything a man seeks Moses had: possessions, pleasure, power, prestige, and prosperity. But Moses turned them all down. He would not trade heavenly things for earthly things.

The world will offer your kids the treasures of Egypt. We must teach them to esteem the things of Christ rather than enjoy the things of this world. The worst we endure for Jesus is of more value than the best the world has to offer.

Moses lived some 1500 years before Christ. Yet he esteemed the reproach of Christ greater than Egypt's riches. How did Moses know about Christ? How did Moses accept Christ? By faith, Moses looked forward to Christ, as we, by faith, look back to Christ.

Amram and Jochebed set the example for Moses. Their words and their actions were consistent. They were not fooled by the world, and neither was Moses.

Parents, don't let the world's disguise fool you; don't let Satan dupe you. When you buy into the disguise of Satan and the world, you will develop the wrong value system. This will be devastating to your children and cause you as a parent to give your children:

- Cars instead of character.
- Clothes instead of chores.
- Conveniences instead of conviction.
- Independence instead of integrity.
- MTV instead of meaning.
- Popularity instead of purity.
- Rights instead of responsibility.

- Stuff instead of Scripture.

- Toys instead of teaching.

Amram and Jochebed raised Moses to not be fooled by the disguises of Satan and the world.

Parents, be wise to Satan's strategy and temptations. Satan will come against the will of God, the Word of God, and the worship of God.

Regarding the will of God, Moses *"refused to be called the son of Pharaoh's daughter"* (vs. 24). Regarding the Word of God, Moses choose to *"suffer affliction . . . than to enjoy the passing pleasures of sin"* (vs. 25). Moses refused to disobey the Word of God. Regarding the worship of God, by refusing the opportunity to become Egypt's next pharaoh, Moses refused to set himself up as a god. The pharaoh was viewed as the incarnation of Ra, the chief Egyptian god.

By the way, Jesus was tempted in the same way. Satan tempted Jesus regarding the will of God by telling Jesus to turn stones into bread. Satan tempted Jesus regarding the Word of God by quoting Scripture out of context. He told Jesus to throw Himself down from the pinnacle of the temple and that angels would attend Him. Satan tempted Jesus regarding the worship of God by offering Jesus all the kingdoms of the earth if only Jesus would worship him.

Parents must teach their children that Satan will put on many disguises and tempt them and bring into question the will of God, the Word of God, and the worship of God.

3. The death of this world

The Scripture says that *"it is appointed for men to die once, but after this the judgment"* (Heb. 9:27). Parents who have faith raise their children and prepare them for eternity.

God instructed Moses regarding the tenth plague which would break the back of Egypt and bring the release of the Hebrews. By this time Moses was a great and popular man. His name rang out in every Egyptian and Jewish home. He was viewed as the deliverer and savior of the Hebrew people. He was successfully overcoming the powerful pharaoh. Moses was indeed the most popular and powerful man on the earth.

Surely Moses, as God's chosen leader and deliverer, would be exempt from the Passover requirements. Yet the Scripture says that, *"by faith he kept the Passover and the sprinkling of blood, lest he who destroyed the firstborn should touch them"* (vs. 28). The greatness of Moses did not exempt him or eliminate the need he had for the blood of the lamb. Moses stood in as much need as did the most vile of persons.

At the burning bush, Moses had previously accepted God's plan to deliver the Jews. Now he must accept God's provision to do so--the blood of lambs. In delivering the Jews from Egypt, God sent ten plagues. The tenth and final plague was administered by the death angel. He would kill the firstborn of every home where there was no blood on the doorposts. The Jews, including Moses, would cover the doorposts and lintel with the blood from a sacrificial lamb. This was an act of faith and obedience. God's plan was to save the Jews. God's provision to save them was the blood of sacrificial lambs, a provision that would save them from death.

Like Moses, we must accept God's plan and God's provision. God's plan instructs us what He wants to do, which is to save us. God's provision instructs us how He will save us, by the blood of Jesus. Death is as sure as life, yet God has provided for us a way of escape. He sent His Son, Jesus Christ, who is the Lamb of God. On the cross He became our sacrifice. On the cross, He shed His blood. It's no wonder that the scripture instructs us that Jesus was the Lamb slain from the foundation of the world (Rev. 13:8). It's no wonder John the Baptist introduced Jesus by saying,

"Behold! The Lamb of God who takes away the sin of the world!" (Jn. 1:29).

Just as the Jews applied the blood to their doorposts and lintel, we must apply the blood of Lamb to our lives. Apart from this blood there is no forgiveness of sin.

Egypt did things their way and died. The Jews did things God's way and lived. The Proverb writer said,

"There is a way that seems right to a man, But its end is the way of death" (Prov. 14:12).

There are ways that seem right to a man: good works, baptism, church attendance, catechism, giving charitable donations, etc. The Bible says these are the way of death. But faith accepts God's provision. Faith accepts the work of Jesus Christ on the cross. This is God's way, and it is the way of faith.

Parents, have you led your children in the way of faith? The greatest joy of parents is to lead their children to believing faith in Jesus Christ.

> *The greatest joy of parents is to lead their children to believing faith in Jesus Christ.*

Parents, your children will face the dangers of this world, the disguise of this world, the death of this world, and . . .

4. The difficulties of this world

Just as Moses experienced difficulties, we will experienced difficulties in this life, especially if we are in a position to lead people.

When the Jews left Egypt, they left with the spoils of Egypt. As they journeyed away from Egypt, Pharaoh stewed over his defeat and humiliation. The longer he thought about it, the more upset it made him. So he mobilized his army and pursued the Jews. When the rear guard of the Jews saw the pursuing Egyptians, their shouts of victory turned into cries of defeat.

By the time the Jews reached the Red Sea, the Egyptians were on their rear flank. The Jews were trapped. At that point, the people lost heart and complained to Moses.

Then they said to Moses, "Because there were no graves in Egypt, have you taken us away to die in the wilderness? Why have you so dealt with us, to bring us up out of Egypt? Is this not the word that we told you in Egypt, saying, 'Let us alone that we may serve the Egyptians?' For it would have been better for us to serve the Egyptians than that we should die in the wilderness" (Ex. 14:11-12).

Whose faith do we see here? It certainly wasn't the faith of the Jews. With the first sight of danger they were willing to go back to Egypt and live as slaves again. It was Moses who had faith.

And Moses said to the people, "Do not be afraid. Stand still, and see the salvation of the LORD, which He will accomplish for you today. For the Egyptians whom you see today, you shall see again no more forever. The LORD will fight for you, and you shall hold your peace" (Ex. 14:13-14).

It was Moses who held up his rod and the waters of the Red Sea parted. Even then it took much faith to walk through the Red Sea with its waters piled up on each side. But the Hebrew writer records, *By faith they passed through the Red Sea as by dry land, whereas the Egyptians, attempting to do so, were drowned* (vs. 29).

Some three million Jews were blessed because of the faith of Moses, which was passed on to him by his parents. What reward for parents to see the faith that they handed down to their children being used to bless other people.

Parents, your children will face the dangers of this world, they will face the disguise of this world, they will face the death of this world, and they will face the difficulties of this world. And they cannot make it to the other side without faith.

Moses would teach us that faith will take you places you have never been before. The only way the Jews could get from Egypt to the Promised Land was by faith.

You see, Egypt represents the world. The Promised Land represents heaven. The only way your children will ever get from this world to heaven is by faith.

The only way your children will ever get from this world to heaven is by faith.

Moses learned of faith through the example and teaching of his parents, Amram and Jochebed. Where will your children get the faith they need to deal with the demands of this life? Where will your children get the faith they need to get to heaven?

What Are the Needs of Our Children?

There are many things in life that we want to influence and shape. A businessman wants to shape his company; a coach want to shape his team; a politician wants to shape his community; a preacher wants to shape his congregation; a teacher wants to shape his students; and a nation wants to shape the world.

But the one thing that demands our attention, our utmost, and our shaping is our children! We exert much energy to change those things outside our home, but exert little effort in changing those things inside the home.

Our world seems to be crumbling beneath our feet because our families are falling apart. It is the responsibility of parents to instruct, develop, and monitor children.

God did not give children to schools, day care centers, youth groups, and churches - He gave them to parents! Therefore, it is parents who will stand and give an account to God for the upbringing of children.

There are three things that children need from parents to shape them as God intended.

1. Our children need boundaries.

Children need boundaries, yet many families today are suffering from bad leadership. Children now run many households, dictating to the parent what to do. A parent who permits this is courting disaster.

To begin with, a parent needs to clearly define and communicate what the boundaries are. Once boundaries have been established, parents should defend them! As a parent, you have the right to expect your child to obey and live by the standards of your home. When disobedience takes place, discipline becomes necessary. If you do not discipline, if you give in to your child, your child will grow up thinking there are no consequences for his wrong choices. Boundaries are important, but if you create them you must defend them. Your words and your actions must be consistent with each other.

Wise Solomon said,

"For whom the LORD loves He corrects, Just as a father the son in whom he delights" (Prov. 3:12). "He who spares his rod hates his son, But he who loves him disciplines him promptly" (Prov. 13:24). And, "The rod and rebuke give wisdom, But a child left to himself brings shame to his mother" (Prov. 29:15).

Discipline is important because it communicates that we love our children. After all, God disciplines His children. If discipline communicates love, and it does, my mom must have been crazy about me. Mom would say as she was whipping me, "I'm doing this because I love you."

Boundaries are important because they keep a kid headed in the right direction.

In my growing up years my mom had boundaries for my brothers and me. I remember one evening when I left home for a date, mom told me what time to be home. When that time passed she called my girlfriend's house to tell me to get home, which was an embarrassment to me. When I arrived home my mom had a suitcase waiting on me and told me in no uncertain terms if this was going to be my response to her instructions, to pack my bags and try living on my own. I assured her that I would, from that point on, obey her rules. My mom was serious about what she said to me, which forced me to get serious about obeying her.

My mom told my twin brother and me that we had to join the youth choir at church. We didn't want to join the youth choir at church, so mom gave us a choice; we could either join the youth choir or take ballet lessons. Well, look out choir, here come the Taylor boys! Mom didn't always give us what we wanted, but she did give us what she thought we needed.

Thinking about my mom reminds me of the police recruit who was asked during an exam, "What would you do if you had to arrest your own mother?" He answered, "Call for backup."

Dr. Adrain Rogers once said about parenting, "It used to be at night that we would bring the children in and put the dog out. Now, we turn the kids loose and bring the dog in."

We need to establish boundaries because children are like wet cement. The longer you wait, the harder the job will be. You can mold and shape cement while it is still wet. But once it hardens and sets up you can do nothing to alter it except take a jackhammer to it.

As a parent don't strive to be your child's best friend. They can, and will, find friends, but there is only one person who can be their mom or their dad. And, Buster, that is you!

Listed below are the twelve rules for raising delinquent children which was published by the Houston, Texas, police department in 1950.

1. Begin in infancy to give your child everything he wants. In this way, he will grow to believe the world owes him a living.

2. When he picks up bad words, laugh at him. This will make him

think he is cute. It will also encourage him to pick up "cuter" phrases that will later blow off the top of your head.

3. Never give him any spiritual training. Wait until he is twenty-one and then "let him decide for himself."

4. Avoid use of the word "wrong." It may develop a guilt complex. This will condition him to believe, later, when he is arrested for stealing a car, that society is against him, and he is being persecuted.

5. Pick up everything he leaves around--books, shoes, and clothing. Do everything for him so he will be experienced in throwing all responsibility onto others.

6. Let him read any printed matter he can get his hands on. Be careful that the silverware and drinking glasses are sterilized, but let his mind feast on garbage.

7. Quarrel frequently in the presence of your child. In this way he will not be too shocked when the home is broken up later.

8. Give a child all the spending money he wants. Never let him earn his own. Why should he have things as tough as you had them?

9. Satisfy his every craving for food, drink, and comfort. See that every sensual desire is gratified. Denial may lead to harmful frustration.

10. Take his side against neighbors, teachers, and policeman. They are all prejudiced against your child.

11. When he gets into real trouble, apologize for yourself by saying, "I never could do anything with him."

12. Prepare for a life of grief. You will be apt to have it.

Our children need boundaries.

2. Our children need beliefs.

Ever since the Separation of Church and State ruling was made by the Supreme Court in 1962, anything that had to do with Christianity has been taken out of the American classroom. No longer can we tolerate prayer, Bible reading, or the Ten Commandments in our schools. We are now training our children in a moral vacuum environment. The consequences of that decision have been devastating. Since that time abortions have increased, teen suicide rates have increased, single-parent families have increased, births to unmarried women have increased, daily television viewing has increased, child abuse has increased, number of crimes committed has increased, average prison sentences have decreased, and SAT scores have decreased.

America is courting self-destruction. A country without God is a country without hope. We no longer have any beliefs or resolve. How did we get from where we used to be as a God-fearing country to a society that no longer has any moral beliefs?

Perhaps the following, which I received by e-mail but know not its origin, says it best:

I think it started when Madeline Murray O'Hare complained she didn't want any prayer in our schools. And we said OK.

Then someone said you had better not read the Bible in school. The Bible that says, "Thou shalt not kill, thou shalt not steal, and love your neighbor as yourself." And we said OK.

Dr. Spock said we shouldn't spank our children when they misbehaved because their little personalities would be warped and we might damage their self-esteem. And we said an expert should know what he's talking about so we won't spank them anymore.

Then someone said teachers and principals had better not discipline our children when they misbehave. And the school administrators said no faculty member had better touch a student when they misbehave, because we don't want any bad publicity, and we surely don't want to be sued. And we accepted their reasoning.

Then someone said let's let our daughters have abortions if they want, and they won't even have to tell their parents. And we said that's a grand idea.

Then some wise school board member said since boys will be boys and they're going to do it anyway, let's give our sons all the condoms they want, so they can have all the fun they desire, and we won't have to tell their parents they got them at school. And we said that's another great idea.

Then some of our top elected officials said it doesn't matter what we do in private as long as we do our jobs. And we said it doesn't matter what anybody, including the President, does in private as long as we have jobs and the economy is good.

And the entertainment industry said let's make TV shows and movies that promote profanity, violence and illicit sex. And let's record music that encourages rape, drugs, murder, suicide, and satanic themes. And we said it's just entertainment and it has no adverse effect and nobody takes it seriously anyway, so go right ahead.

Now we're asking ourselves why our children have no conscience, why they don't know right from wrong, and why it doesn't bother them to kill strangers, classmates, or even themselves.

Undoubtedly, if we thought about it long and hard enough, we could figure it out. I'm sure it has a great deal to do with "we reap what we sow."

Our children and our society need boundaries and beliefs.

Solomon said,

"Train up a child in the way he should go, And when he is old he will not depart from it" (Prov. 22:6).

We must note here that Solomon instructs parents to train children, not tell children. You know the old saying, "Do as I say, not as I do." That philosophy will produce many unsuccessful parents and unruly children.

Parents are to *"Train up a child in the way."* *"The Way"* is a New Testament term used for Christianity. Five times in the Book of Acts the term, *"The Way,"* is used for Christianity (Acts 9:2; 19:9, 23; 24:14, 22). Parents are responsible and accountable to raise their children in *"The Way."*

The paraphrase of Proverbs 22:6 is, "As the twig is bent, so is the tree inclined." Infant trees are planted with their trunk attached to three guy-wires to make sure they grow straight. If you wait too long you'll never be able to influence the growth of that tree.

There are three guy-wires that every parent should attach to their young children in order to train them in the way they should go.

Parents should train their children:

1) In contemplation.

This deals with the mind. Parents must teach their children to fix their minds on Christ. The educational system emphasizes the priorities of the world and wants children to succeed in this world. Christian parents should desire for their children to succeed in the next world.

The apostle Paul said,

"Do not be conformed to this world, but be transformed by the renewing of your mind" (Rom. 12:2). He also said we are to "have the mind of Christ" (1 Cor. 2:16).

A child has no hope to behave correctly until he first believes correctly. One's beliefs will determine one's behavior.

2) In compassion.

This deals with the heart. Every child is born with the capacity to love, to hate, to laugh, to cry, to hope, or to despair. Parents must instill in their children, by consistent and persistent means, a fear of sin and a faith in the Savior.

The best way I know to instill a love for Jesus in your children, is for your children to see a love for Jesus in you.

3) In conviction.

This has to do with the will and the conscience. Parents must train the will of children in obedience. Parents must command respect and obedience because parents stand in the place of God in the lives of their youngsters.

A conscience can be either seared or sensitive. This is why it is essential that a child's conscience be guided by the Word of God. The condition of one's conscience will determine one's conviction, and one's conviction will determine one's conversion.

If a child ends up no-account, lazy, rebellious, a thief, or a fornicator, it should be in spite of the parents' training, not because of, or lack of, the parents' training.

As parents we are to instill in our children right beliefs. That won't happen if we are not in the Word of God. Proverbs says much about giving your children righteous instruction and a godly belief system. Solomon in all his wisdom knew that child-rearing was certainly an area that we need much wisdom.

The hardest thing I've have ever done, or attempted to do, is to raise children. It's even harder than pastoring a church.

Principles for raising a . . . C.H.I.L.D.

Choices

Parents are to teach children that life is full of choices. Good choices mean good consequences; bad choices mean bad consequences. It's the law of the harvest: You reap what you sow.

Heart

Parents are to train their children to build their lives on the Word of God. The psalmist said,

"Your word I have hidden in my heart, That I might not sin against You!" (Psa. 119:11).

Intellect

Parents are to teach their children to think right and not like the world. Paul said,

"Finally, brethren, whatever things are true, whatever things are noble, whatever things are just, whatever things are pure, whatever things are lovely, whatever things are of good report, if there is any virtue and if there is anything praiseworthy--meditate on these things" (Phil. 4:8).

Loyalty

Parents should raise their children to be loyal, to be devoted, to be faithful to Jesus as Lord of their lives. Parents should also teach their children to be loyal to their spouses and faithful to their church.

Parents should teach their children to do the right thing simply because it is the right thing to do. This means teaching them to see tomorrow, not just the gratification of today. Doing the right thing builds character. Teach them that if they wait until the feeling is right, before they do right, they will accomplish little in life.

Determination

Parents should teach their children to be determined to stand alone if necessary. They should teach them to be like Daniel, who took a stand because he *"purposed in his heart that he would not defile himself"* (Dan. 1:8).

One of the great tragedies in our country today is that we don't believe anything anymore. My Granny use to tell my brothers and me, "If you don't stand for something, you'll fall for anything."

Any parent who neglects the first part of Proverbs 22:6, which says, *"Train up a child in the way he should go,"* cannot claim the second part, which says, *"And when he is old he will not depart from it."*

Our children need boundaries and our children need beliefs.

3. Our children need blessings.

Our kids need the blessing of their parents. Just as God blesses us, we need to bless our children.

> "Blessed be the God and Father of our Lord Jesus Christ, who has blessed
> us with every spiritual blessing in the heavenly places in Christ" (Eph. 1:3).

How can we bless our children? Let me offer the following suggestions:

1. By loving God. The greatest blessing you can give your children is to be men or women of God. Again from Solomon we get these words,

> "Most men will proclaim each his own goodness, but who can find a
> faithful man? The righteous man walks in his integrity; His children are
> blessed after him" (Prov. 20:6-7).

2. The second greatest blessing you can give your children is to

love each other. This provides security and stability in their lives. It is disturbing to our kids when we parents don't get along.

3. Understand that your children are on loan from God. Ultimately they are His, not yours. Therefore, raise them in a godly manner so that when you give the finished product back to God, both you and He will be pleased.

4. Raise your children to be who and what God made them to be--not what you want them to be.

Solomon said, *"Train up a child in the way he should go,"* not "in the way you want him to go."

God is not really interested in our boys becoming great athletes nor our girls becoming cheerleaders. He is interested in them becoming all He has designed them to be.

5. Allow your children to dream. Don't douse their fire. As 12-year olds in Sunday School, we were asked what we wanted to be when we grew up. Most of the kids said "doctor, fireman, nurse, etc . . . " I said, "I'm going to be a pro football player." As a kid, I thought I would replace Johnny Unitas as the quarterback for the Baltimore Colts. My mom knew that it was unlikely for me to replace Johnny Unitas, but she let me dream. My dreams used to be based on me and the flesh; now my dreams have matured so that they are based on God and my faith.

6. Read the Bible and pray with your children often. We should pray for our kids, and we should pray with our kids.

7. Take them to church with you. Your children need to witness your involvement in the church and see you worship the Lord. When children are young they will follow your advice, but when they are old they will follow your example.

8. Don't buy into the lie that you can substitute quality time for quantity of time. When you give your kids time and attention, you communicate, "You are important to me."

9. Don't expect your children to be perfect, but do expect them to strive for excellence. Have two rules for your children: Do what's right, and do your best.

10. Tell your kids you love them and are proud of them. Generally, children want to please their parents. In the second grade I bought mom a pair of earrings for 5 cents. Every time mom would clean the house on Saturdays, she would wear those earrings. I was so proud that I had given mom something that pleased her so much.

11. Even in difficult times, trust God and His grace to be sufficient in their lives. Remember what Paul said,

"But where sin abounded, grace abounded much more" (Rom. 5:20).

12. Touch your kids, hug your kids, and kiss your kids. In this way they feel loved.

There is something special about a parent blessing his/her children. Isaac blessed Jacob instead of Esau (Gen. 27). Although Jacob tricked Esau, the Bible tells us that Esau *"despised his birthright"* (Gen. 25:34). Jacob blessed Joseph (Gen. 48:15), and he also blessed Joseph's sons, Manasseh and Ephraim. But in doing so he crossed his hands and put his right hand on the younger, Ephraim, instead of the older, Manasseh.

Most of us will not be remembered for being president of the United States, or a Nobel Prize winner, or someone who invented a cure for cancer. However, in the hearts of our children, we can be forever remembered as parents who loved Jesus, who loved each other, and who greatly influenced and impacted our children by giving them boundaries, beliefs, and blessings.

The Blowup of America

The dictionary defines a "blowup" as an explosion. A forest fire fighter would describe a "blowup" as a manageable forest fire which erupts into a raging inferno. This kind of blowup can burn thousands of acres in just a matter of a few minutes.

A "blowup" would be an appropriate way to define our culture today. America finds itself at the top, or near the top, of the world in murder, rape, drug use, divorce, abortion, child abuse, and births to unwed mothers.

What was once a more manageable situation in America, has now erupted into a raging inferno.

We see the flames when we watch television and see the traditional family ridiculed. We hear the fire's crackle when we pick up the morning newspaper and read that another young person is missing, or has been raped and murdered. Or when you are single and feel as if there's not another single person out there who shares your values of having a God-centered relationship. Or when you are deciding where to send your kid to school and safety issues outweigh academic issues. You smell the smoke when most of your friends are now divorced, or many of your coworkers are homosexual. You feel the heat when you are in a blended marriage and your ex-spouse troubles you over the custody of your children, the discipline of your children, or the education of your children.

The inferno rages and the greatest nation in the world is on the verge of self-destruction. You know you're near a blowup when you have to fight to insure that legislation is passed to correctly define marriage as being between a man and a woman.

What causes a blowup? There are three elements present in a blowup: fuel, fire, and oxygen.

Let us look at these three elements and how they contribute to the blowup of our society.

1. The fuel in this blowup is the loss of devotion.

That which fuels a cultural blowup is when society no longer has a respect and reverence of God. America used to have a devotion to God and biblical principles.

How can we say we're devoted to God, yet declare that it is illegal to read the Bible in public or that we can no longer post the Ten Commandments? To reject the Bible is to reject the Author of the Bible.

How can we claim devotion to God while we refuse to protect the most helpless among us--the unborn child? How can we claim devotion to God while at the same time sanction homosexual unions?

Let's imagine, for just a moment, that our country was about to be born today. Could you imagine the national outrage if the founding fathers suggested that "In God We Trust" be stamped on the currency of this new nation? It is evident that our founding fathers had a devotion to God and the truth of Scripture. John Adams, our second president said, "Our Constitution was meant for a moral and a religious people. It is wholly inadequate for the governance of any other."

The loss of devotion has attacked our faith.

We have lost our devotion to God, in part because we have lost two other things.

A. We have lost our fear.

Solomon, the wise king of Israel, said,

"The fear of the LORD is the beginning of knowledge, But fools despise wisdom and instruction" (Proverbs 1:7).

The word *"fear"* used here means "reverence." The reverence for God is the beginning of knowledge. We have no hope of knowledge until we first respect and revere God! We try to come across as being sophisticated, but without a reverence for God we are nothing but blooming idiots!

At the core of a moral meltdown is a culture that does not fear God. The fear of God is the basis for all authority and accountability. If there is no God, who has authority to establish the standard for living? Then to whom are we accountable? If we are not accountable to God, to whom are we held accountable? The Republicans? The Democrats? Congress? If we are accountable to no one, then we can do as we please, which is why we are in the shape we are in today.

> *At the core of a moral meltdown is a culture that does not fear God.*

America today resembles what was said of Israel during the days of the judges.

In those days there was no king in Israel; everyone did what was right in his own eyes (Judges 21:25).

When Jesus is not King, everyone will do what is right in their own eyes.

In our culture God is ridiculed and not even recognized, much less revered. It's not surprising there's no fear of God in society, because even in the Christian community we are strangely silent on the subject.

There is little teaching on His judgment of sin, His wrath, or His anger. We have become so politically correct that very little is heard about hell today. Even where we haven't rejected God, we have conveniently reduced Him or recreated Him to our specifications.

The height of human foolishness is to ignore God and His Word and somehow hope for wisdom and a peaceful world.

After World War I, the League of Nations was formed. The League's goals included disarmament, the prevention of war, settling disputes between countries, and improving global welfare. The League's headquarters in Geneva, Switzerland, was referred to as the Palace of Peace. The League had a library of seventy-five thousand books on peace. But the League of Nations could not maintain peace, because God and His Word were ignored. The onset of World War II made it clear that the League of Nations had failed in its purpose.

There is only one book that deals with peace, and it is the only book that God has authored--the Holy Bible!

We now have the United Nations to keep our world safe. The only thing we have learned from history, is that we have learned nothing from history.

Solomon knew what he was talking about when he said, *"The fear of the LORD is the beginning of knowledge, But fools despise wisdom and instruction."*

B. We have lost our facts.

Jesus said, *"If you abide in My word, you are My disciples indeed. And you shall know the truth, and the truth shall make you free"* (John 8:31-32).

Today our society has abandoned absolute truth and traded it for relativism. Today we have only one rule: there are no rules.

The greatest tragedy of our society is that we have lost our respect for truth. Today the absolute has become relative, and the relative has become absolute. Today we don't have truth, we have only interpretation. Truth today is only an opinion, and one opinion is as good as another.

Truth has been replaced with tolerance. We tolerate everything in America today except God, God's Word, and God's people.

Who would have thought a few years ago that a court would consider a law suit to remove a cross from a war memorial in San Diego, California?

Jesus said, *"you shall know the truth, and the truth shall make you free."* Truth is true whether you believe it or not. Gravity is true whether you believe in it or not. If you jump off of a skyscraper, you will experience the truth of gravity whether you believe it or not. Whether you accept Jesus Christ or not, one day you will experience the truth of His judgment!

2. The fire in this blowup is the loss of dignity.

When you lose your fear of God, the natural progression is to lower your standard and lose your values.

The loss of devotion has attacked our faith.

The loss of dignity has attacked our families.

Today our families, and the family structure, are under attack. Once God is out of the way there is no standard for our conduct. Without a God to please, we have only ourselves to please. With the spiritual man out of the way, we live to gratify the physical man.

We have so lowered the standards today that we no longer believe that the two-parent (one woman and one man) family is necessarily best. Such thinking is misguided tommyrot!

Divorce is destroying our children. When the nest is broken, the eggs will crack. We have created a moral climate today that not only accepts divorce, but expects it.

When the nest is broken, the eggs will crack.

Divorce is also destroying our culture. We have become a culture of divorce. And there is an awkward silence concerning the social consequences of divorce. Even the church is hesitant to confront this issue. Why the silence? Because most of us have either divorced, or know close relatives or friends who have divorced, and we don't want them to feel as if we are condemning them. Yet God says that He hates divorce (Mal. 2:16).

The family is under attack! During the 1990s the bipartisan National Commission on Children wrote, "The unmet needs of American youngsters is a national imperative as compelling as an armed attack or a natural disaster." [1]

The attacks of September 11, 2001, brought the devastation of property and life. Americans rallied in support by giving millions of dollars and praying for those who suffered.

When hurricane Katrina hit the Gulf coast in August of 2005, it devastated the whole region and took many lives. Americans once again rallied in support. Thousands of people went to lend aid, millions of dollars were donated, and untold multitudes interceded in prayer.

Yet today we have a far worse disaster than these. It is the destruction of marriages, the desertion of children, and the disintegrating of the family structure. Where is the outcry? Why aren't Americans rallying like we did when we were attacked, or when we suffered a natural disaster? The answer is--we have lost our reverence for God and, consequently, we have lowered our standards.

When God is removed as the supreme object of our worship, we find something else, or someone else, to worship. We turn to idol worship. When you no longer worship the Creator, you end up worshiping the creation.

The apostle Paul put it this way,

"Therefore God also gave them up to uncleanness, in the lusts of their hearts, to dishonor their bodies among themselves, who exchanged the truth of God for the lie, and worshiped and served the creature rather than the Creator, who is blessed forever. Amen. For this reason God gave them up to vile passions. For even their women exchanged the natural use for what is against nature. Likewise also the men, leaving the natural use of the woman, burned in their lust for one another, men with men committing what is shameful, and receiving in themselves the penalty of their error which was due. And even as they did not like to retain God in their knowledge, God gave them over to a debased mind, to do those things which are not fitting" (Romans 1:24-28).

Idolatry leads to immorality. When a man rejects the truth he accepts *"the lie."* What is this lie? The lie is that man is his own god and should worship and serve himself, not the Creator. It is the same lie that Satan used in the Garden to deceive Eve.

When you believe *"the lie"* you do that which is *"against nature"* and that which is *"not fitting."* Here Paul is speaking about the sin of homosexuality. Notice the words Paul uses here to describe homosexuality: *"uncleanness . . . dishonor . . . vile passions . . . shameful . . . debased . . . not fitting."*

To have a debased mind means that one is incapable of making right judgments. The reason a homosexual uses his body in a perverted way is because he is perverted in his thinking.

According to the Bible, homosexuality is not simply an alternative to heterosexuality. It is a sin that, if not corrected, will invoke the wrath of God!

The family is not only under attack by homosexuality, but also by feminism. The feminist movement has blurred the distinction between masculinity and femininity. This gender blending causes us not to recognize the roles of men and women, and creates social confusion.

It is rare that happily married women are among feminist leaders. It has been estimated that some forty percent of the National Organization of Women is lesbian.

One day while driving down the road, I followed a woman driving the car in front of me. She had two bumper stickers on her car. One read, "Women are natural born leaders. You're following one now." The other bumper sticker read, "Hell was full so I came back."

The Bible knows nothing about the idea of women's lib or the inferiority of women. Since God has made us *"male and female"* (Gen. 1:27), we should recognize our differences and appreciate them. The problem with both homosexuality and feminism is that you can't fool Mother Nature. Trying to fool Mother Nature is to risk spiritual death. Mother Nature knows that marriage and family are not a life-style choice, like choosing what color car you want to purchase. Marriage and family is the rock on which all of human existence stands.

3. The oxygen in this blowup is the loss of decency.

To be decent is to be free from vulgarity or immodesty. Decent would not describe our culture where anything and everything goes. We live in a culture where people's individual freedoms of expression have stepped over the line.

John Underwood, a writer for the Miami Herald wrote, "Civilizations do not give out, they give in. They come apart, not in a flash, but by the inch. In a society where anything goes, everything eventually will." [2] Cal Thomas, syndicated columnist, speaking of the entertainment industry wrote, "They have not only abandoned my values, they now have sunk to the sewer level, dispensing the foulest of smells that resemble the garbage I take to the curb twice a week" [3]

The loss of devotion has attacked our faith. The loss of dignity has attacked our families.

The loss of decency has attacked our future.

When respect for God is gone, the outgrowth will be the lowering of standards. The lowering of standards will invoke the judgment of God, which will affect our future. When devotion is gone, dignity is soon to follow. And when dignity is gone, decency is soon to follow.

In Genesis 18, we see Abraham interceding for Lot and his family by bargaining with God. Abraham knew that God would judge Sodom. Abraham knew more about Sodom's future than did the citizens of Sodom.

How did Abraham know about Sodom's future? God told him. The Lord said,

"Shall I hide from Abraham what I am doing?" (Gen. 18:17).

I believe God's righteous people understand much more about the future of America than do the politicians in Washington D.C. God's people understand that

"Righteousness exalts a nation, but sin is a reproach to any people" (Prov. 14:34).

The city of Sodom was wicked. The citizens there had given themselves over to sexual behavior that was contrary to nature. They would not repent, and they would not even conceal their perverted practices.

Abraham was burdened for his nephew Lot who lived in Sodom, so he began to intercede for Lot by bargaining with God. What would it take for God to spare the city? How many righteous people would it take to save Sodom?

Abraham asked God if He would spare the city for fifty righteous people. Then forty-five . . . then forty . . . then twenty . . . then ten (Gen. 18:24-32). Abraham stopped at ten. I wonder why he stopped there? Until Abraham arrived at the number ten, he was assured by God that He would spare the city. But when Abraham arrived at the number ten, he stopped there because he had arrived at the divinely set number.

There comes a time when God draws the line and says that's enough! For the city of Sodom it was ten. I've often wondered what the divine limit is for America?

> *There comes a time when God draws the line and says that's enough!*

The people of Sodom must have thought that Abraham was odd, old fashioned, and a religious fanatic because he lived by a much higher standard than they did.

People who live for Christ are looked upon with disapproval and skepticism. The people of Sodom did not know, nor did they appreciate, what they owed to those who were righteous. God had been patient with the city of Sodom for some time, but all the while the number of those righteous began to shrink to such low levels that it crossed God's divine limit. It was at that time that God *"rained brimstone and fire on Sodom,"* (Gen. 19:24) and annihilated the city and its inhabitants.

Why would Abraham intercede and ask God to spare such a wicked people? Wouldn't the world be better off if these unrighteous people were gone? Abraham did not want to see these people die separated from God and be lost forever.

Abraham knew that God was *"not willing that any should perish but that all should come to repentance"* (2 Pet. 3:9). Abraham knew that God *"desires all men to be saved and to come to the knowledge of the truth"* (1 Tim. 2:4). Abraham knew that *"the wages of sin is death"* (Rom. 6:23), and that on the other side of death is an eternal hell.

Never underestimate the importance of believers in a society. And as a believer, never underestimate the importance of your witness. If Lot had led just a few folks to the Lord, the city could have been spared. Our witness is important to God and it is important to society, even if society never acknowledges or appreciates it.

We must fight indecency in our country! Many have resolved that redeeming our nation is impossible. They have given up, thinking the battlefront is too large and the problems are so overwhelming.

For the future of our children, grandchildren, and unborn generations yet to come, we must go till He comes, give till we drop, preach till everyone knows, and work till He stops us. For future generations we must not look back, let up, slow down, back away, or be still. We must not give up, shut up, or let up until we have prayed up, worked up, and extinguished the blowup. So help us God!

1. Fortune, August 10, 1992, 34.

2. John Underwood, "How Nasty Do We Wanna Be? Reflections on Censorship and a Civilized Society," Miami Herald, July 22, 1990, IC.

3. Cal Thomas, "TV Continues Slide into Sewer," Human Events, November 24, 1990.

An Inside Look at Adultery

In Matthew 5-7 we have what is called "The Sermon on the Mount." It is the greatest sermon ever preached by the greatest preacher to have ever preached, Jesus Christ. In this sermon, Jesus gives us an inside look at adultery. Jesus' teaching was in contrast with the religious leaders of that day. While both agreed that adultery was forbidden and wrong, Jesus' teaching included a wider application of sin than did the religious leaders. Man wants to limit the commands of God to as small an area as possible. Jesus expanded the application of the sin of adultery to include not just the physical and external act of adultery, but also the internal attitude of our heart.

The mistake Israel's religious leaders made is the same one we make today and that is to think that sin is an external act only. Jesus, in dealing with murder and now with adultery, goes to the heart of the problem by going to the problem of the heart.

Jesus said,

"You have heard that it was said to those of old, 'You shall not commit adultery.' But I say to you that whoever looks at a woman to lust for her has already committed adultery with her in his heart. If your right eye causes you to sin, pluck it out and cast it from you; for it is more profitable for you that one of your members perish, than for your whole body to be cast into hell. And if your right hand causes you to sin, cut it off and cast it from you; for it is more profitable for you that one of your members perish, than for your whole body to be cast into hell" (Matthew 5:27-30).

From Jesus' words let us consider three things:

1. The deed of adultery

Jesus had just finished His teaching on murder and the sixth commandment. Now He focuses on adultery and the seventh commandment which says,

"You shall not commit adultery" (Ex. 20:14).

The sixth commandment protects the sanctity of life.

The seventh commandment protects the sanctity of marriage.

Let us consider ten aspects of adultery:

A. *The definition of adultery*

What is adultery? Adultery usually means a married person having sexual relations with someone not his or her spouse. Fornication is a term used to describe the sexual act between unmarried people.

However, sometimes in Scripture adultery applies to all sexual relations with someone who is not your married partner regardless of whether you are married or not. Such is the case here in the Sermon on the Mount.

This teaching of Jesus is not just for married people, but teaching that applies to all.

B. *The depravity of adultery*

The Scripture teaches us that adultery is evil. When Joseph was tempted by Potiphar's wife to commit adultery, Joseph responded by saying,

"How then can I do this great wickedness, and sin against God?" (Gen. 39:9).

Joseph said that adultery was *"great wickedness."* Adultery is no trivial sin! It is *"great wickedness"* and a *"sin against God."*

The adulterer is unclean. His eyes sparkle with lust. His heart burns like a furnace in unclean desires. The Scripture says of the adulteress,

> For a harlot is a deep pit, And a seductress is a narrow well. She also lies in wait as for a victim, And increases the unfaithful among men (Prov. 23:27).

The world calls adultery by watered down names like an "affair" or "alternative life-style" or "live-in marriage" or a "trial marriage" or even "love." This is lust, not love.

Joseph had it right. It is *"great wickedness."*

C. The deceit of adultery

Adultery is deceitful and promotes dishonesty. Adultery is often spoken of as "unfaithfulness" and it is. It is unfaithfulness to the marriage vows.

Immorality is inseparably connected with deceit. When David committed adultery, he then began to try to cover up his sin by deceit.

D. The disease of adultery

All kinds of sexually transmitted diseases come from adultery. Speaking of sexual sin the Proverb writer said,

> And you mourn at last, When your flesh and your body are consumed (Prov. 5:11).

Despite the reality of AIDS and twenty other sexually transmitted diseases, today's youth continue to try sex at earlier and earlier ages. Today 35% of 15-year-old boys, and 27% of 15-year-old girls have had sexual intercourse. Each year over 3 million teenagers contract a sexually transmitted disease.

This year 10 million teens will engage in 126 million acts of intercourse producing one million pregnancies, 406,000 abortions, 134,000 miscarriages, and 490,000 births.

Why are our youth taking such risks? Because they are looking for love. When you teach your kids right from wrong; when you pray with your kids; when you take you kids to church; when you have restrictions for your kids, they may act like they don't like it but they do. Because it communicates that you love them!

Paul wrote,

> Flee sexual immorality. Every sin that a man does is outside the body, but he who commits sexual immorality sins against his own body (1 Cor. 6:18).

E. The divorce of adultery

Nothing ruins a marriage like adultery. Adultery populates the divorce courts. Purity is a must for a good marriage. Today the average marriage lasts seven years.

According to *U.S. News and World Report*, the United States is at the top of the world for divorce. "Till death do us part" has been changed to "Till something better comes along." Today, America is called a post-martial society.

Adultery destroys trust and what marriage can go the distance without trust.

F. The degrading of adultery

Adultery destroys the dignity and degrades a person. Jumping from partner to partner is an animalistic thing to do. Even some animals have more judgment than do some humans.

The dove is loyal to its mate. The stork is loyal to its mate. In fact, if a stork leaves his own mate and joins with another, the rest of the storks fall upon him and pull his feathers out.

G. The debt of adultery

Immoral conduct is expensive.

For by means of a harlot a man is reduced to a crust of bread; And an adulteress will prey upon his precious life (Prov. 6:26).

The prodigal son spent his inheritance in *"riotous"* living (Lk. 15:30 KJV). The word literally means "unsavedness." When he returned home his older brother said to their father about his younger brother,

"This son of yours . . . has devoured your livelihood with harlots" (Lk. 15:30).

H. The dishonor of adultery

The worst thing about the sin of adultery is that it dishonors God. When David confessed his adultery with Bathsheba, he said,

"Against You, You only, have I sinned, And done this evil in Your sight" (Psa. 51:4).

All sin is primarily against God. It is true that adultery is against others as well, but sin is always first and foremost against God.

Adultery dishonors God but it also dishonors the one involved. Whoever commits adultery with a woman lacks understanding; He who does so destroys his own soul. Wounds and dishonor he will get, And his reproach will not be wiped away (Prov. 6:32-33).

A soldier's wounds for his country are full of honor. A martyr's wounds for Christ are full of honor. But the wounds of an adulterer are full of dishonor.

I. *The death of adultery*

Adultery breeds death. After David's adultery with Bathsheba, he had Uriah, Bathsheba's husband, killed in order to cover up his sin.

Many abortions-the death of unborn babies-are the result of immoral relationships.

J. *The damnation of adultery*

The sin of adultery damns the soul of the adulterer or adulteress.

Do you not know that the unrighteous will not inherit the kingdom of God? Do not be deceived. Neither fornicators . . . nor adulterers, nor homosexuals, nor sodomites . . . will inherit the kingdom of God (1 Cor. 6:9-10). Marriage is honorable among all, and the bed undefiled; but fornicators and adulterers God will judge (Heb. 13:4).

While repentance does keep the soul from hell, there is a sense in which Divine judgment comes upon every adulterer. It is a sin that will damn the sinner on earth as no other sin.

2. The desire of adultery

Jesus said,

"But I say to you that whoever looks at a woman to lust for her has already committed adultery with her in his heart" (Matt. 5:28).

Notice here the words of Jesus. He says, *"I say to you."* Listen up now, this is Jesus speaking, not the religious leaders. Jesus is now asserting His authority over that of the religious leaders and their tradition.

We note two things here.

A. *The gazing of our eyes*

Jesus said, *"whoever looks at a woman to lust"* commits adultery. This is not an incidental glance, but an continuous, intentional gazing.

Jesus is talking about an intentional look with the purpose of lusting. He is speaking of a man who looks in order to satisfy his evil desire. He is speaking of the man who goes to an adult bookstore to look lustfully. He is speaking of a man who selects a certain movie or TV channel for its sexual orientation. He is speaking of the man who goes on the internet with a lustful purpose.

Looking at a woman lustfully does not cause a man to commit adultery. Jesus said he *"has already committed adultery with her in his heart."*

It's not the lustful look that causes the sin in the heart, but the sin in the heart that causes the lustful look. The lustful look is but an expression of the heart. The heart is the soil where the seeds of sin are imbedded.

> *It's not the lustful look that causes the sin in the heart, but the sin in the heart that causes the lustful look.*

Jesus is not speaking of unexpected and unavoidable exposure to sexual temptation. When a woman is inappropriately dressed, Satan will surely try to use that to tempt a man with lustful thoughts. But there is no sin if the temptation is resisted, and you turn your eyes in another direction and dismiss the sight from your mind. It is the continuous looking in order to satisfy lustful desires that Jesus is condemning.

David was not at fault for seeing Bathsheba. She was obviously bathing in such a location that he could not help but see. It could be that she wanted King David to see her. David's sin was that he gave in to that lustful temptation and looked at her without looking away and putting the experience out of his mind. The fact that he brought her to his chambers expresses the immoral desire in his heart.

Arthur Pink said, "If lustful looking is so grievous a sin, then those who dress and expose themselves with the desire to be looked at and lusted after . . . are not less but perhaps more guilty. In this matter it is not only too often the case that men sin but women tempt them to do so."

B. The guarding of our heart

To avoid sexual sin, we must guard our heart. Job said,

"I have made a covenant with my eyes; Why then should I look upon a young woman?" (Job 31:1).

Job knew that sin begins in the heart and that he was just as deserving of God's punishment for looking at a woman lustfully as for committing adultery with her. He therefore determined in advance to guard his heart by making *"a covenant"* with his eyes not to gaze at a woman.

An adulterous heart plans to EXPOSE himself or herself to lustful situations. The godly heart plans to ELUDE himself or herself from lustful situations. An adulterous heart PROCURES for himself or herself lustful materials. The godly heart PROTECTS himself or herself from lustful materials.

Like Job, we must make a covenant with our eyes and every other part of our body and mind to shun lust and pursue purity.

3. The deliverance from adultery

In verses 29 and 30, Jesus gives us instruction so that we can be delivered from adultery. But our deliverance is dependent upon our obedience.

Let us consider five aspects regarding our obedience:

A. The preservation of obedience

Jesus said, *"If your right eye causes you to sin, pluck it out and cast it from you"* (Matt. 5:29). The word *"sin"* here means "to stumble or offend." If something offends you or causes you to stumble in the area of sexual sin, we are to *"pluck it out and cast it from"* us. In other words, get rid of it. Your preservation is of a higher priority than keeping that which damns you.

Amputation is better than damnation. If a part of our body that was diseased was fatally threatening the rest of our body, we would have that part removed by amputation to preserve our life.

B. The pain of obedience

Amputation is not without great pain. You may have to do some very painful things to keep you from adultery. But purity is worth the pain. A greater pain than any amputation is the pain of losing your purity.

C. The parts of obedience

Jesus here refers to the *"right"* eye and the *"right"* hand. This does not mean that the left eye or left hand will not be a problem. The emphasis on the *"right"* focuses on what is of the most value, or dearest to us.

The right eye is the eye most people use to shoot a gun or to shoot an arrow. The right hand is the most valuable because most people are right handed.

Jesus is saying no matter how important something is, if it causes us to sin we are to cut it off.

D. The principle of obedience

The principle Jesus is teaching here is that we are to take strong action against anything that would be a snare and lead to sexual sin.

The right eye and the right hand represent those things which are especially ensnaring for adultery.

We must separate and isolate ourselves from anything that can ensnare us in sexual sin. That may mean you will have to cut off some friendships, some subscription to a magazine, your membership at the video store, cable TV, or the internet.

The action you need to take may seem severe, but here Jesus is advocating severe action. It takes severe action to combat a serious sin.

E. The priority of obedience

Jesus is teaching us three important priorities here:

1. We are to put the ETERNAL over the EVERYDAY.

Jesus says it is better to suffer in this life than in the next life. We had rather suffer loss in this life than to suffer in eternal hell.

2. We are to value our SOUL over the SENSUAL.

Jesus says it is better to lose body parts than it is to lose your soul. The care of the body is not nearly as important as the care of one's soul.

3. We are to put PURITY over PLEASURE.

Jesus says that we are to emphasize our soul's purity over our body's pleasure. Holiness is the way to true happiness. To sacrifice purity for pleasure will make you a loser every time. Adultery will give temporary physical pleasure, but it destroys purity and that destroys true and lasting pleasure.

Since adultery starts in the heart, guarding your heart must be your top priority.